Phonics **Fundamentals**

Volume 2

Contents

Congratulations on your purchase of some of the finest teaching materials in the world.

Author: Jo Ellen Moore
Illustrator: Joy Evans
       Kathleen Morgan
Editor: Bob DeWeese
Graphics: Michelle Tapola

Evan-Moor
HELPING CHILDREN LEARN

Short Vowel Words

A Review

Section One

D0555493

Where do we begin?

It is important to remember that students need to experience success in learning to read. So before we introduce a new skill, we must allow students adequate practice in the skills previously taught. This section is designed to provide review of short vowel sounds and practice in blending.

Before a student begins this chapter, he/she should have been introduced to:
- Consonant letter names and sounds
- Short vowel sounds
- Blending of sounds into words

cat	pet	hit	top	hut
had	set	sit	hop	cut
sat	net	pit	pop	but

- Writing the letters of the alphabet

If your students are comfortable with blending, we will have some fun reviewing short vowel sounds on the following activity sheets. This gives learners the opportunity to practice decoding sounds both in isolation and in short sentences. It is an exciting moment for learners when they realize they can build words with sounds and they can do it all by themselves.

This chapter introduces a small number of sight words that students will need to know.

a	blue
the	green
red	brown
yellow	black
orange	

Color the Puzzle

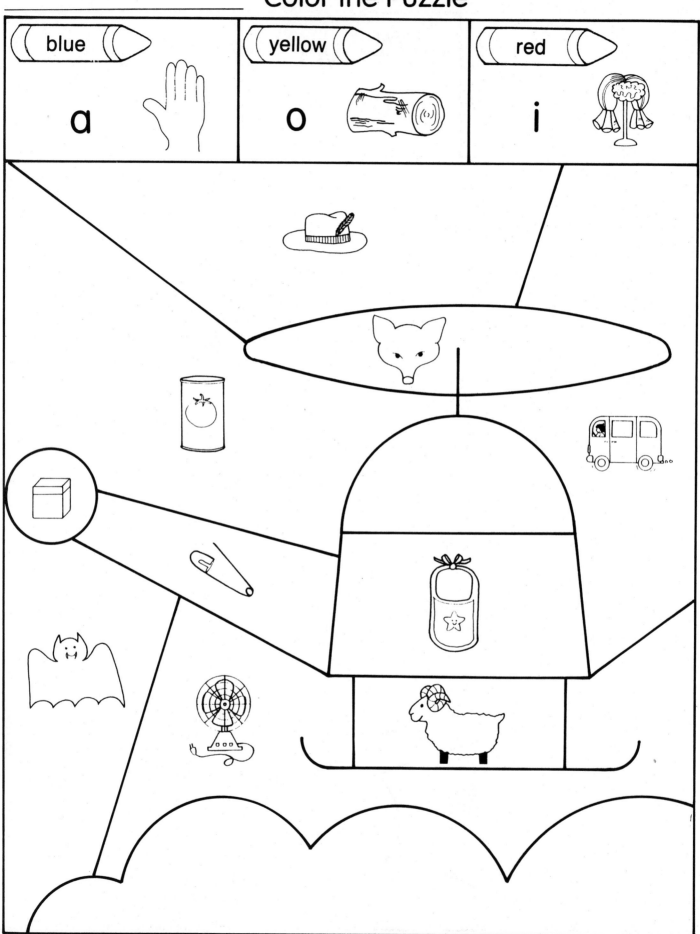

Color the Puzzle

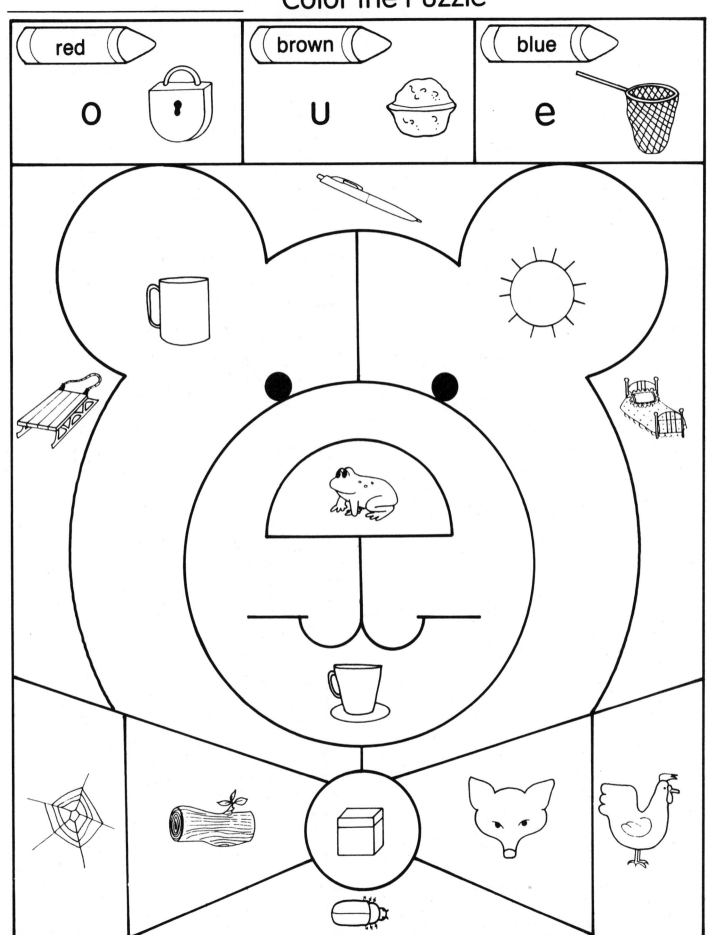

5

Phonics Fundamentals II

Color the Puzzle

Color	brown o 🦊	yellow a 🐱
blue e	white u	red i

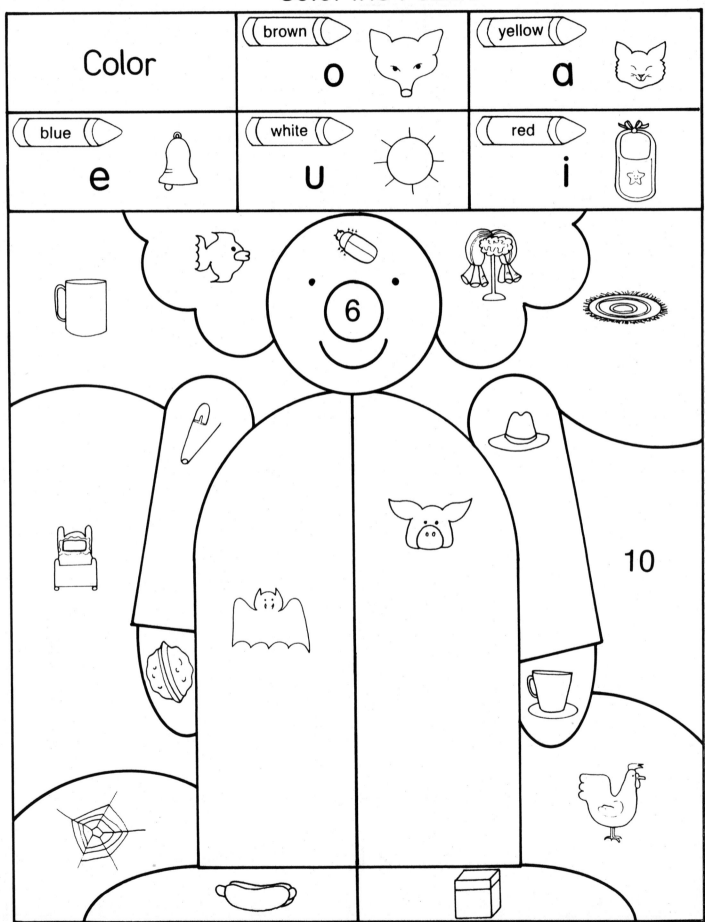

Phonics Fundamentals II

Name_____

Write the Missing Letter

_an

_an

_an

_ig

_ig

_ig

_en

_en

_en

a b c d e f g h i j k l m n o p q r s t u v w x y z

Phonics Fundamentals II

Name _____

Write the Missing Letter

___og

___ox

___um

___at

___et

___ug

___un

___eb

___ut

a b c d e f g h i j k l m n o p q r s t u v w x y z

Phonics Fundamentals II

Name_____

Write the Missing Letter

b_d

s_x

t_b

m_p

b_x

c_p

c_p

l_g

p_g

a   e   i   o   u

9

Name _____

Write the Missing Letter

m __ n   l __ g   s __ n

r __ g   r __ t   h __ n

b __ b   w __ b   t __ p

a   e   i   o   u

Phonics Fundamentals II

Name _____

Write the Missing Letter

ca___   bu___   ja___

tu___   ne___   fo___

li___   ju___   to___

a b c d e f g h i j k l m n o p q r s t u v w x y z

Name_____

Write the Missing Letter

ha___

bo___

10
te___

di___

we___

lo___

cu___

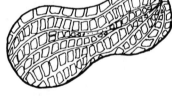
nu___

do___

a b c d e f g h i j k l m n o p q r s t u v w x y z

Name _____

Write the Missing Letter

fa___

l___d

___ub

ca___

g___m

___us

___un

b___t

___ib

___am

___og

p___n

Phonics Fundamentals II

Name_____

___an

n__t

he___

s__n

ba___

___id

be___

___op

w__g

___up

si___

j__t

Name_____

Match:

ant

egg

pin

jet

bag

run

net

cot

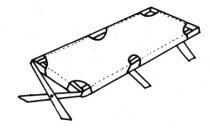

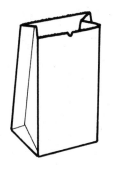

Name_____

Match:

web

hat

men

wig

log

gum

bug

van

Phonics Fundamentals II

Name _____

Match:

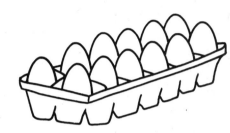

hot dog

cub hug

hot sun

big dog

pig pen

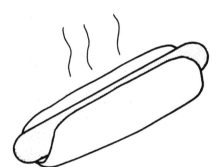

cat bed

egg box

ant hill

Phonics Fundamentals II

Name _____ Write:

 _____	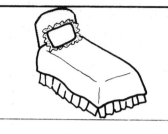 _____	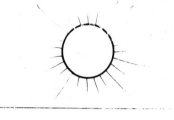 _____
 _____	 _____	 _____
 _____	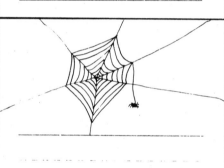 _____	 _____
 _____	 _____	 _____

bed	pig	man	cap
top	fan	nut	web
bus	rat	hen	sun

Phonics Fundamentals II

Name _____ Write:

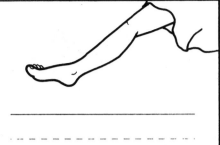

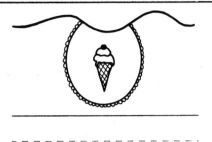

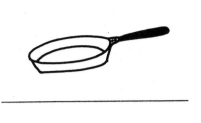

_____
- - - - - - - - - - - -
_____

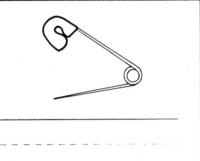

_____
- - - - - - - - - - - -
_____

_____
- - - - - - - - - - - -
_____

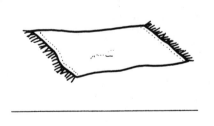

_____
- - - - - - - - - - - -
_____

bib	fox	cub	rug
hat	pan	pin	cat
six	ant	can	leg

     Phonics Fundamentals II

Name _____ Write: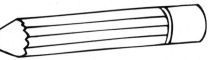

jug	pan	jam	cap
wig	van	egg	cub
hill	leg	bug	ten

Phonics Fundamentals II

Name _____

Write: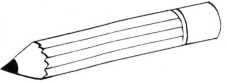

a _____ in a _____

a _____ in a _____

a _____ in a _____

a _____ on a _____

a _____ in a _____

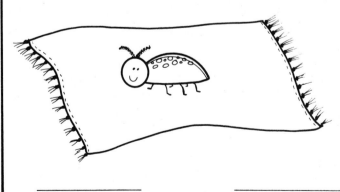

a _____ on a _____

21   Phonics Fundamentals II

Match:

a rat on a hill

an egg in a pan

a hat on a man

a dog on a log

a bat in a net

a dog in a bed

Phonics Fundamentals II

Name _____ Write: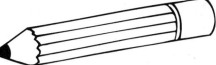

The dog can dig.   Tom sat on the bed.

The fox hid.   The pig got a nut.

Nan can mop.   The hen got an egg.

23   Phonics Fundamentals II

Name _____

Match:

The cat is fat.

The dog can run.

The fox is red.

The bed is big.

The man is hot.

The ant sat.

Phonics Fundamentals II

Read and draw:

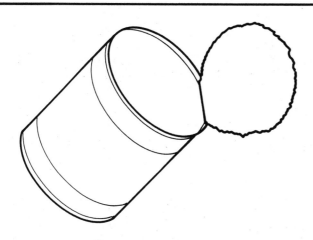

red jam in the can

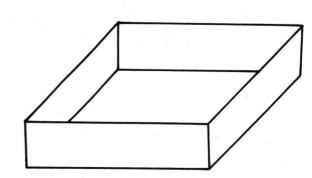

an egg in the box

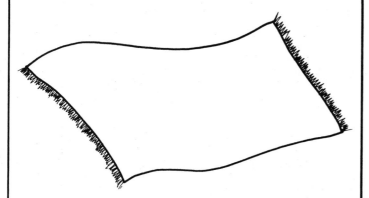

dots on the rug

a hat on the man

a cat on the bed

a pig in the pen

Name _____

Cut and paste:

Pat sat in the sun.	Sam is in bed.
Tom got the cat.	The fox ran up the hill.
The pig is in the mud.	The box is on the rug.

       Phonics Fundamentals II

Name_____

Match:

The bus is big.

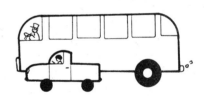

Tom got the gum.

Sam got jam on the bib.

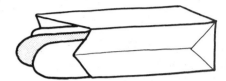

The pig is in the mud.

Dot sat on the cat.

The hot dog is in a bag.

Name_____

Read and draw:

1. a big box
2. a top in the box
3. ten red dots on the top

1. a red cup
2. a fan on the cup
3. an egg in the cup

   Phonics Fundamentals II

Name_____

Unscramble

acn

_____
- - - - - - - - -
_____

abg

_____
- - - - - - - - -
_____

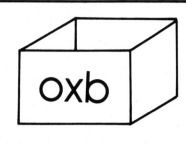

oxb

_____
- - - - - - - - -
_____

tah

_____
- - - - - - - - -
_____

tab

_____
- - - - - - - - -
_____

pcu

_____
- - - - - - - - -
_____

otp

_____
- - - - - - - - -
_____

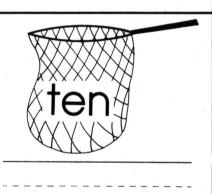

ten

_____
- - - - - - - - -
_____

but

_____
- - - - - - - - -
_____

sbu

_____
- - - - - - - - -
_____

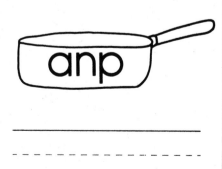

anp

_____
- - - - - - - - -
_____

mgu

_____
- - - - - - - - -
_____

Phonics Fundamentals II

Name_____

Write:

1. run.   Bob   can

_____
- - - - - - - - - - - - - - - - -
_____

2. cat   The   fat.   is

_____
- - - - - - - - - - - - - - - - -
_____

3. A   hid.   fox

_____
- - - - - - - - - - - - - - - - -
_____

4. Sam   wet?   Did   get

_____
- - - - - - - - - - - - - - - - -
_____

5. hot   dog.   the   Fix

_____
- - - - - - - - - - - - - - - - -
_____

6. the   red?   Is   hen

_____
- - - - - - - - - - - - - - - - -
_____

Name_____

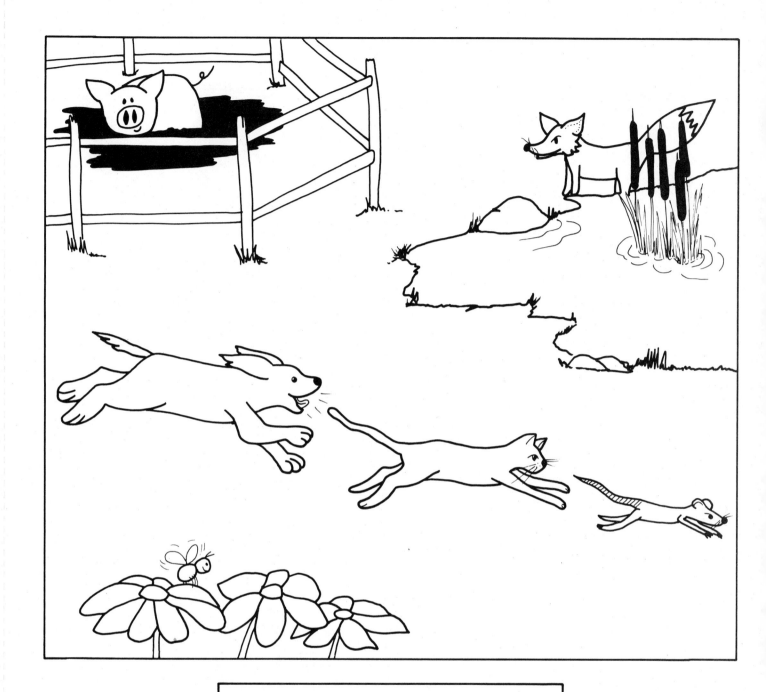

1. The dog is brown.
2. The pig is yellow.
3. The fox is red.
4. The bug is green.
5. The cat is orange.
6. The rat is black.

Phonics Fundamentals II

Read and draw:

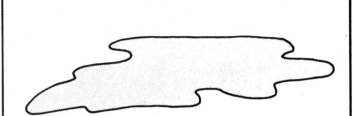

a pig in the mud

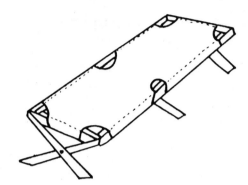

a dog on the cot

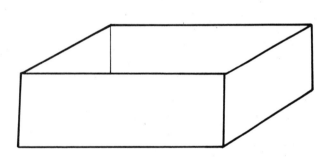

a hot dog in the box

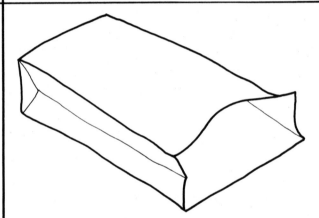

nuts in the bag

a cap on Pat

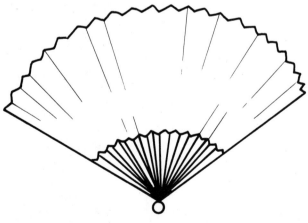

red dots on the fan

 Phonics Fundamentals II

Name _____

yes   no

1. Is the dog big? _____

2. Is the fox in a box? _____

3. Is the ant on the rug? _____

4. Did the cubs hug? _____

5. Did the fox run? _____

6. Did the dog nap? _____

Name _____

yes   no

_____

1. Did the pig get in the mud? _____

_____

2. Is the rat on the mat?

_____

3. Is the pig wet?

_____

4. Did the rat get a rag?

_____

5. Is the bug big?

_____

6. Is a hat on the pig?

               Phonics Fundamentals II

Name _____

1. The _____ hid.

2. A _____ got wet.

3. The _____ ran up the hill.

4. The sun is _____.

5. The man is _____.

6. A fox _____.

| hot |
| man |
| wet |
| hid |
| fox |
| dog |

Name _____

1. The sun is yellow.

2. The hill is green.

3. The egg is blue.

4. The hat is orange.

5. The hen is red.

6. The jet is black.

Phonics Fundamentals II

Name _____

Write:

1. dog   The   big.   is

_____

2. Is   Nan   on   bus?   the

_____

3. sat   on   Dot   cot.   the

_____

4. Ted   get   Did   a   jet?

_____

5. The   wet.   web   is

_____

6. Get   hot   dog.   the   big

_____

Unscramble

Draw a picture here.

mud. got A the in pig

dog had The nap. a

get a Jim Did red hat?

cat ran The and hid.

Phonics Fundamentals II

Introducing Long Vowel Sounds

Aa Ee Ii Oo Uu

We are now ready to introduce the **long** sound of each vowel. A set of pages is provided for each long vowel sound. These pages allow students to listen for these new sounds at the beginning and in the middle of words. Each activity is designed to build confidence and ease in reading.

letter and picture activity card page

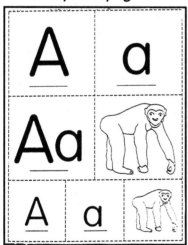

stick puppet to use in practicing sounds

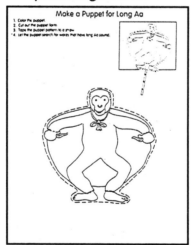

poem emphasizing the letter and its sound

cut and paste page

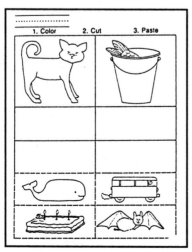

sound search page (beginning sound)

sound search page (medial sound)

Using the Letter and Picture Cards

These cards may be combined with the set of consonant and short vowel cards prepared for the students in *Volume 1* of **Phonics Fundamentals**.

The large-size cards are provided for teacher demonstration. The reproducible small-size flash cards are for students to use for individual practice. A second set of the small-sized cards can be provided for students to practice with at home.

You can use the activities listed below with a small stack of newly-learned letters or with a larger set of letters that have been known for awhile. Either way, start with a demonstration and group participation session. When you are sure they know what they are to do, have your learners practice with their own cards.

Make sure to keep practice sessions SHORT and FUN. Encourage parents to do the same. You want your learners to ask for more, not for you to have to push for more. Celebrate success and effort. Don't emphasize problems.

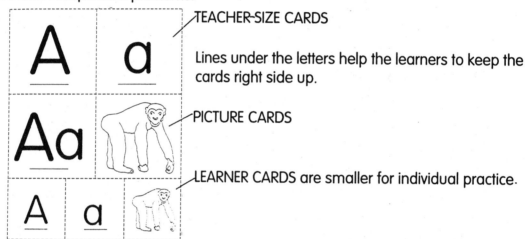

TEACHER-SIZE CARDS

Lines under the letters help the learners to keep the cards right side up.

PICTURE CARDS

LEARNER CARDS are smaller for individual practice.

Ways to use the reproducible cut-out cards:

Show and Tell
A partner holds the cards up one at a time.
The practicer tells what is on each card.

Tell and Show
A partner says a letter name or sound.
The practicer points to the letter or picture.

Match the Sounds
The set of known small letters and pictures is scrambled. The practicer matches the letter with the picture that has the same vowel sound.

Listen for the Vowel
The students have their vowel cards in front of them as the teacher says a word with a long vowel. The student holds up the card that represents the vowel sound in that word.

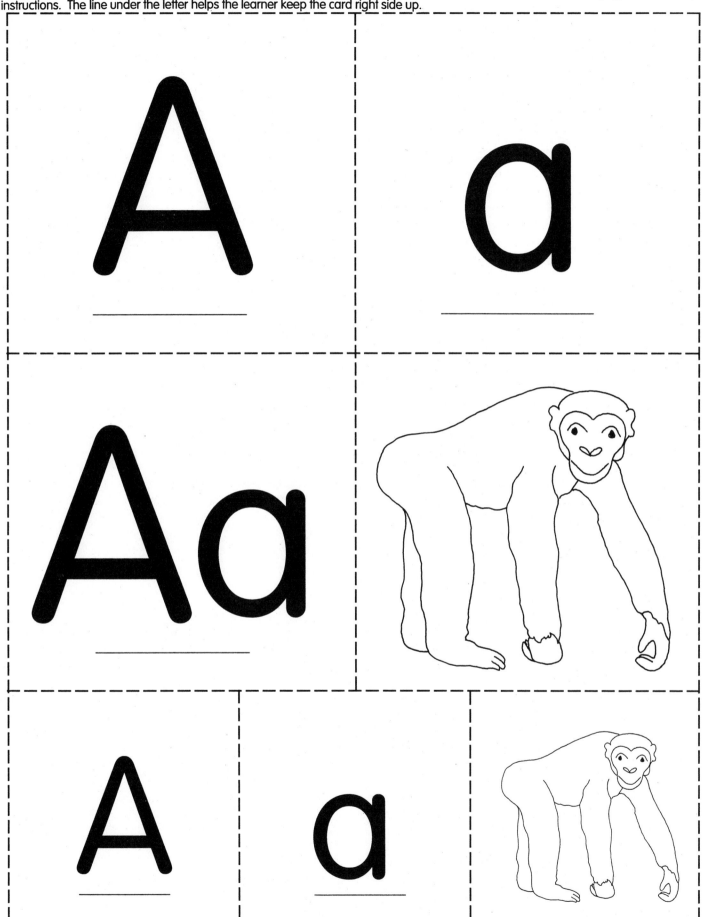

Phonics Fundamentals II

Make a Puppet for Long Aa

1. Color the puppet.
2. Cut out the puppet form.
3. Tape the puppet pattern to a straw.
4. Let the puppet search for words that have long Aa sound.

My ape in
a cape.

Abe, the Ape

Abe, the ape,
   swirled his cape
And danced upon the table.

Then ate the cake
   Kate had baked
As fast as he was able.

Phonics Fundamentals II

Children mark the pictures that begin with the sound of long a.
Answers: acorn apron angel ache

Aa

How many can you find? ☐

name

© 1994 by Evan-Moor Corp.   45   Phonics Fundamentals II

Children mark the pictures where they hear the sound of long a in the middle of the word.
Answers: pail   sail   whale   wave   cake   tail

How many can you find?

Phonics Fundamentals II

Note: Reproduce these activity cards. Large cards are for the teacher's use. Small cards are for the students' use. See page 40 for instructions. The line under the letter helps the learner keep the card right side up.

E

e

_____

_____

Ee

_____

E

e

_____   _____

Make a Puppet for Long Ee

1. Color the puppet.
2. Cut out the puppet form.
3. Tape the puppet pattern to a straw.
4. Let the puppet search for words that have long Ee sound.

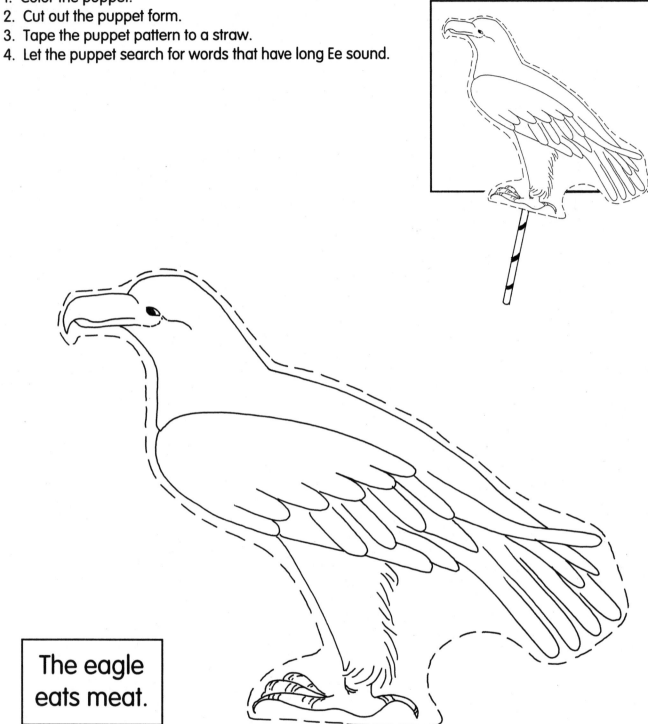

The eagle eats meat.

Steve is "he."
Lee is "she."
I am "me."
All are "we."

1. Color   2. Cut   3. Paste

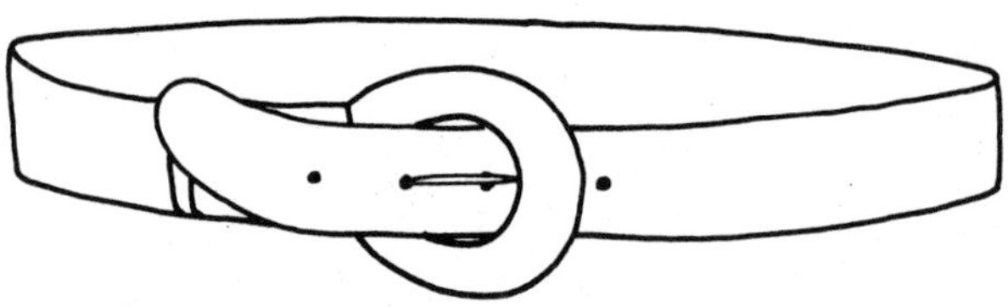

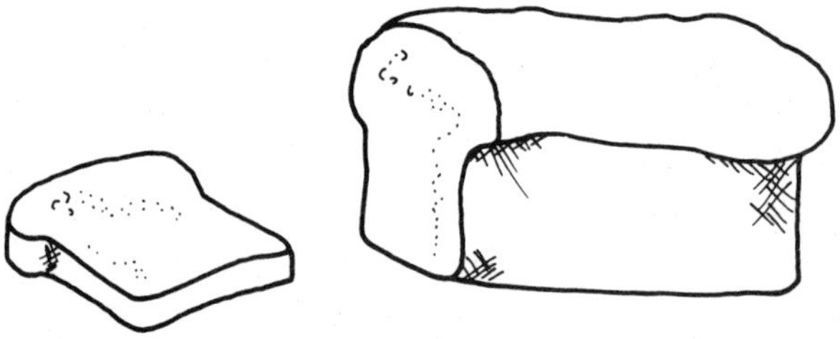

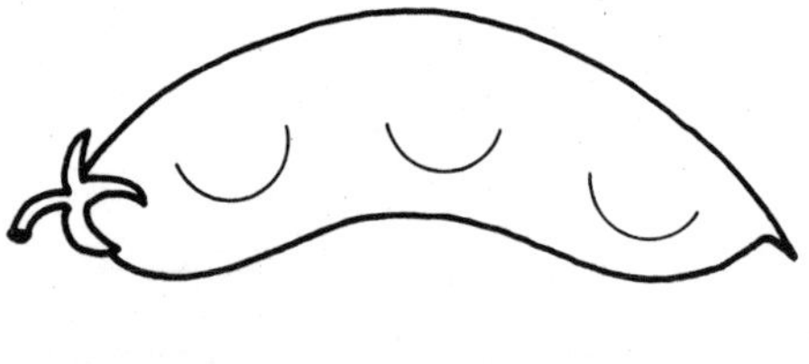

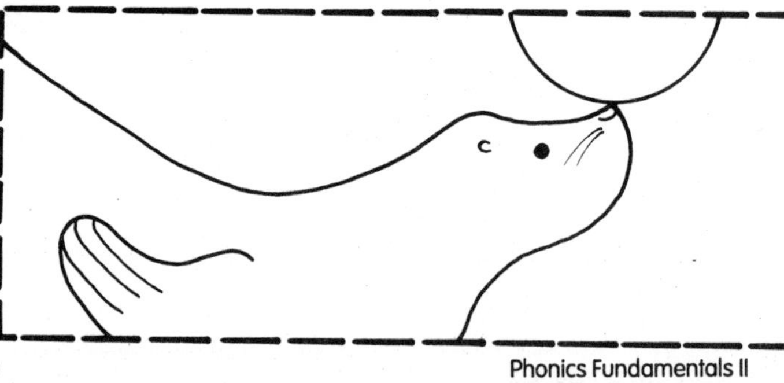

Phonics Fundamentals II

Children mark the pictures that begin with the sound of long e.
Answers: eel   eagle   eat

Ee

name

How many can you find?

Children mark the pictures where they hear the sound of long e in the middle or at the end of the word.
Answers: leaf tree jeep wheel knee feet

Ee

How many can you find? ☐

name

52   Phonics Fundamentals II

Note: Reproduce these activity cards. Large cards are for the teacher's use. Small cards are for the students' use. See page 40 for instructions. The line under the letter helps the learner keep the card right side up.

Make a Puppet for Long I i

1. Color the puppet.
2. Cut out the puppet form.
3. Tape the puppet pattern to a straw.
4. Let the puppet search for words that have long I i sound.

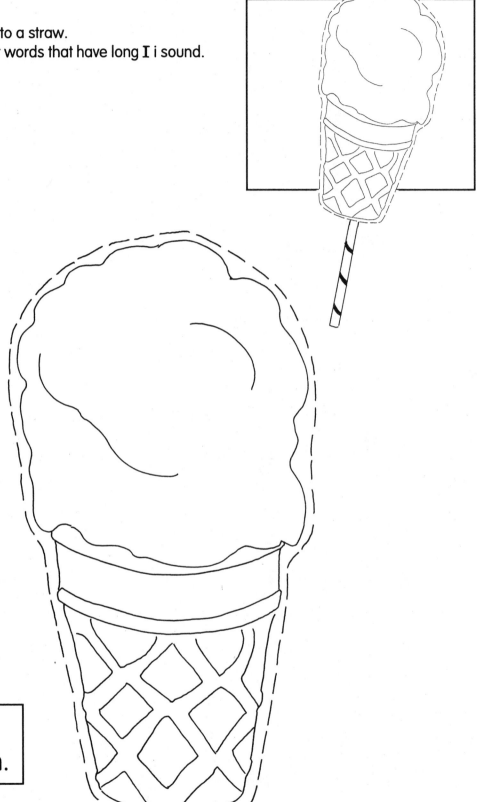

I like
ice cream.

Di and Mike

Di rides her bike.
Mike takes a hike.
I fly my kite.
That's what we like.

55

1. Color   2. Cut   3. Paste

Children mark the pictures that begin with the sound of long i.
Answers: ice cream ice island iron ivy

How many can you find? ☐

Children mark the pictures where they hear the sound of long i in the middle of the word.
Answers: pipe kite bike nine tie pie

Ii

name

How many can you find?

58

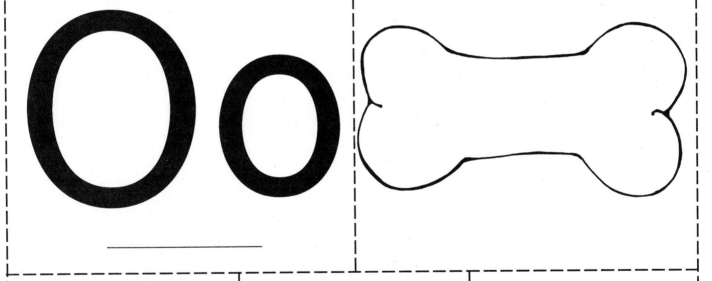

Make a Puppet for Long Oo

1. Color the puppet.
2. Cut out the puppet form.
3. Tape the puppet pattern to a straw.
4. Let the puppet search for words that have long Oo sound.

My Dog Mo
has a busy nose.

My Old Dog Mo

My old dog Mo
Has a busy nose.
She pokes it in holes
Where ever she goes.

1. Color   2. Cut   3. Paste

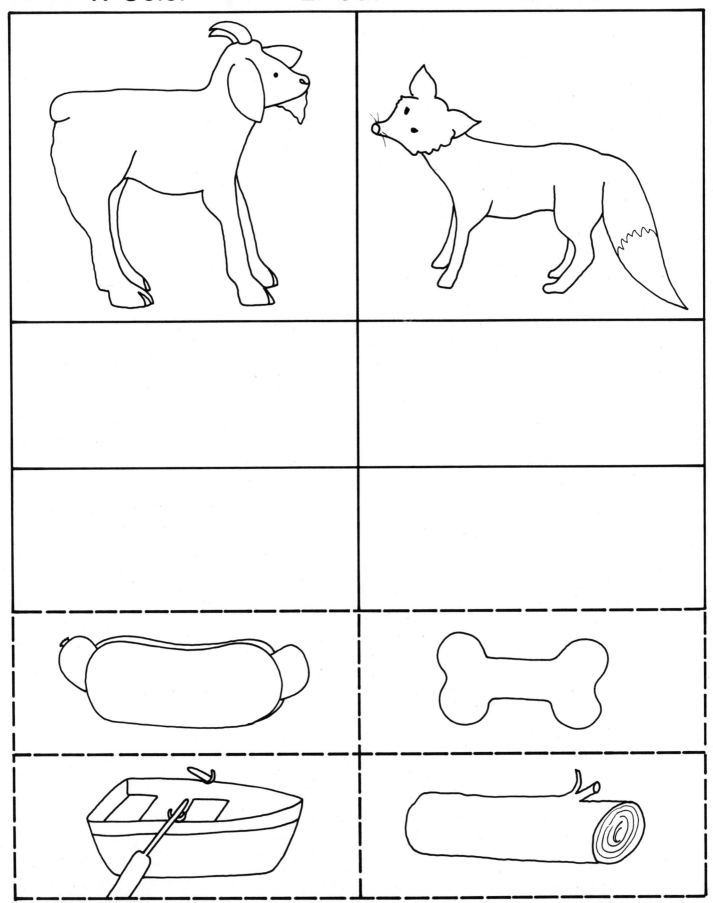

Children mark the pictures that begin with the sound of long o.
Answers: ovals   orangutan   overalls   oar   ocean   over

How many can you find? ☐

name

Children mark the pictures where they hear the sound of long o in the middle of the word.
Answers: boat goat coat toad bone rope road

name

How many can you find?

Note: Reproduce these activity cards. Large cards are for the teacher's use. Small cards are for the students' use. See page 40 for instructions. The line under the letter helps the learner keep the card right side up.

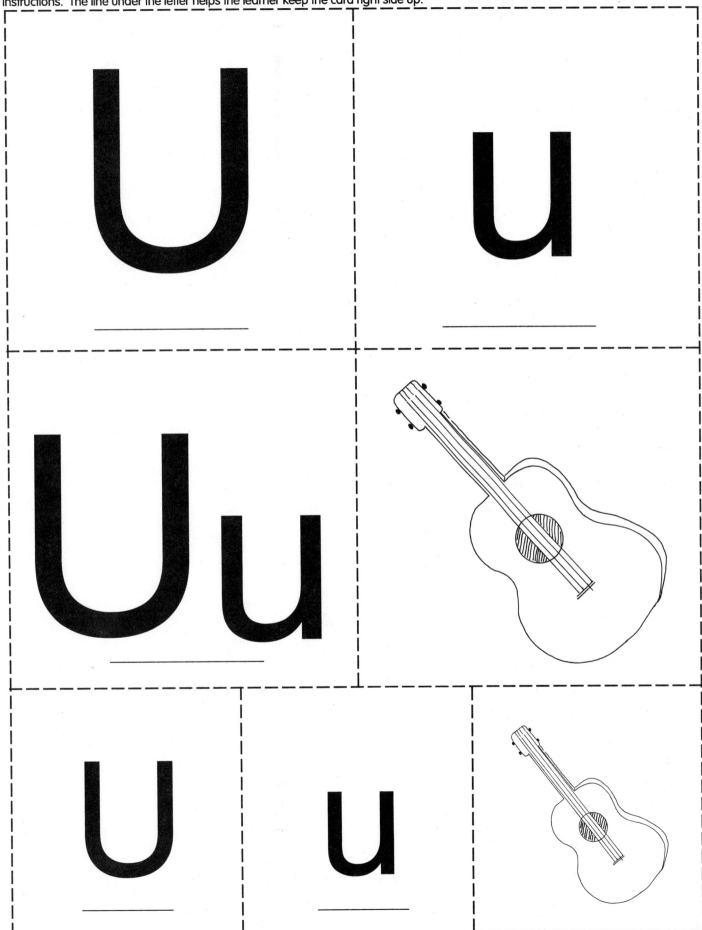

Make a Puppet for Long Uu

1. Color the puppet.
2. Cut out the puppet form.
3. Tape the puppet pattern to a straw.
4. Let the puppet search for words that have long Uu sound.

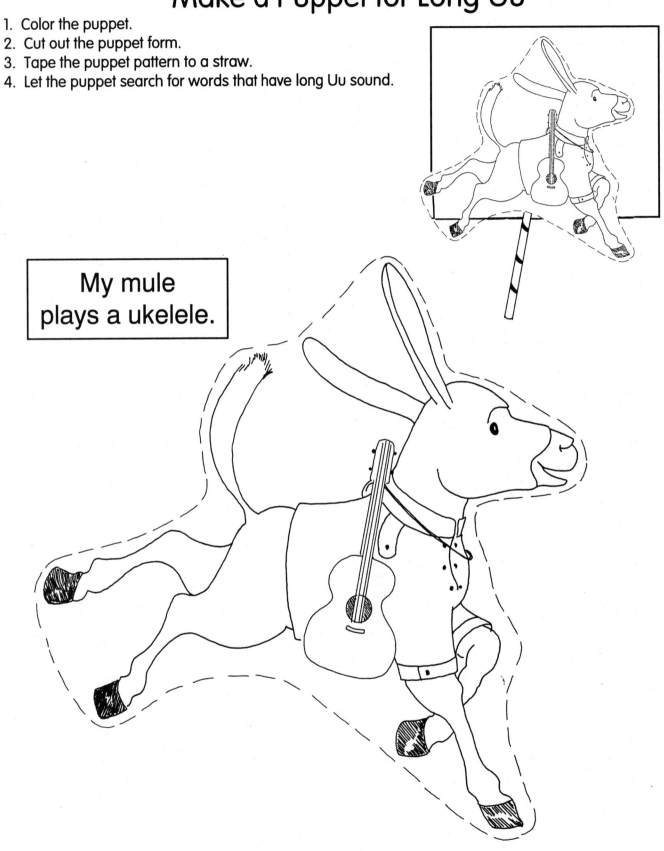

My mule
plays a ukelele.

A Cute Little Mule

A cute little mule
in a uniform
Plays the ukulele
for a unicorn.

1. Color   2. Cut   3. Paste

Phonics Fundamentals II

Children mark the pictures that begin with the sound of long u.
Answers: unicorn unicycle uniform ukulele

U u

How many can you find? ☐

name

Children mark the pictures where they hear the sound of long u in the middle of the word.
Answers: cube mule music

Uu

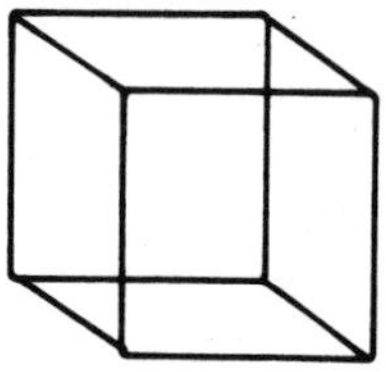

name

How many can you find? ☐

Color the Puzzle

blue	yellow	red
a	o	e

Color the Puzzle

green   a
orange   U
yellow   i

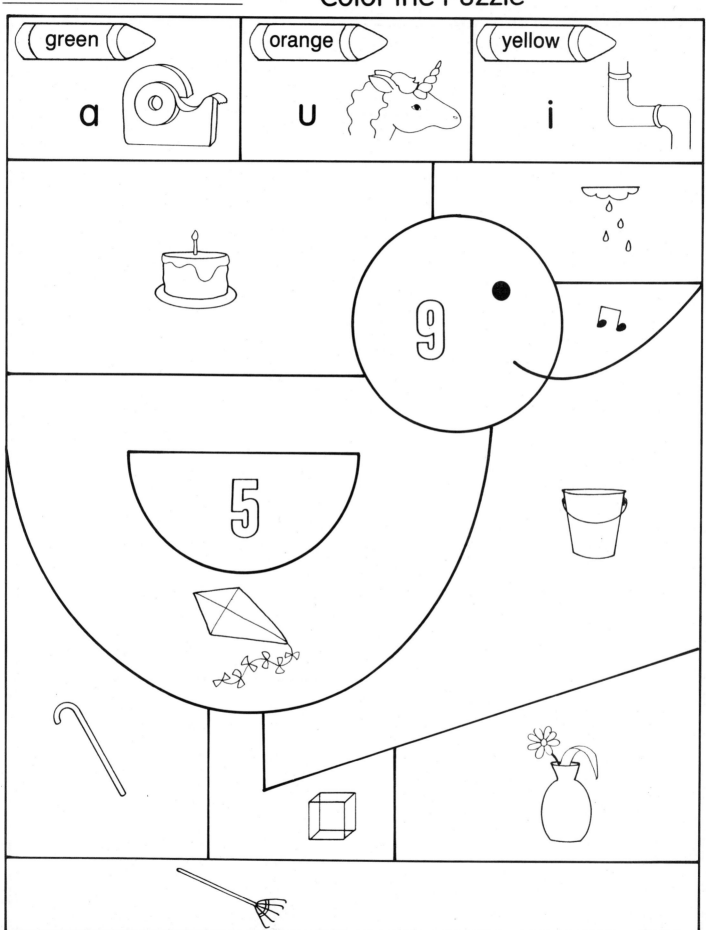

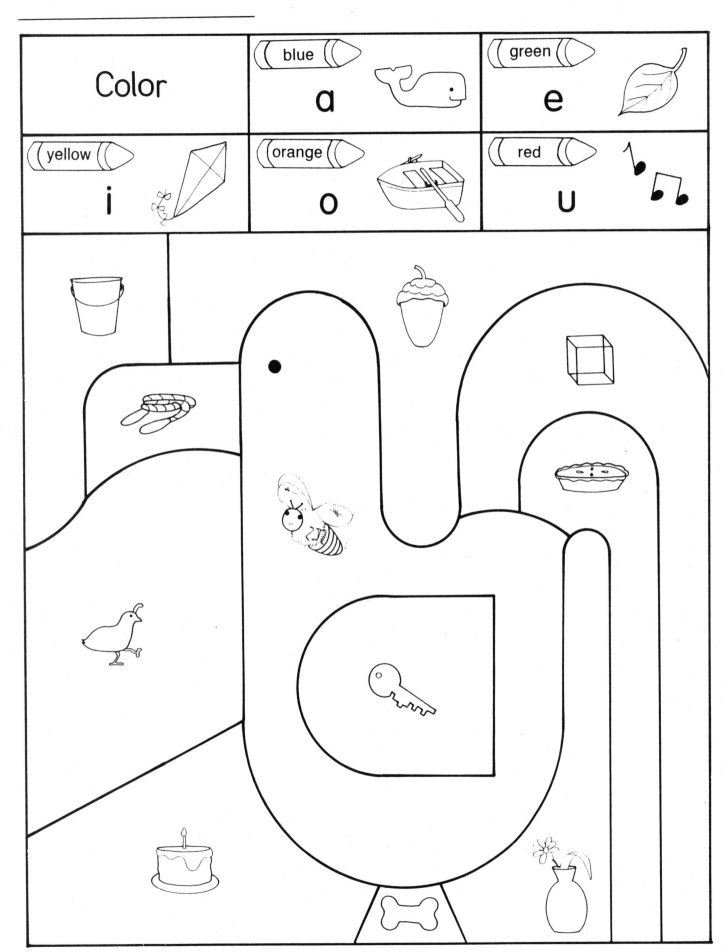

Color | blue <br> a | green <br> e
yellow <br> i | orange <br> o | red <br> u

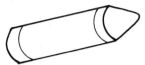

Match the vowel sounds.

1.		2.	
3.		4.	
5.		6.	
7.		8.	
9.		10.	

 Phonics Fundamentals II

What Makes a Vowel Long?

When and Why

There are three cases when a vowel is usually forced to say its long sound:
- at the end of a syllable or at the end of a word
- in the center of a syllable when a silent e comes at the end
- when two vowels sit together but only one speaks; oa as in toad

What is a Syllable?

Make students aware that words are divided into parts called syllables. Give students experience with listening for how many syllables they hear in words. It helps to ask students to clap out these syllables as they are learning to listen for them.

one syllable	two syllables	three syllables
run	happy	champion
jump	shovel	important
hill	singing	possible
pan	cracker	strawberry

Become Aware

As students read more and more, they will begin to recognize that if a syllable has a vowel at the end, it will probably be a long vowel sound. If the vowel is in the center of the syllable, it will probaby be short. Unless.......

Silent e Speaks!

Students like to discover the power of the silent e. Just after we learn that a vowel should be short in the center of a syllable, along comes that silent e and forces the vowel to say its long name. Do some chalkboard work with students to give them experience with this new discovery.

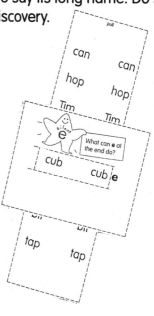

- cap becomes cape
- tap becomes tape
- kit becomes kite
- dim becomes dime
- cub becomes cube

Now you may want to reproduce for your students the *Silent e Word Machine* on the following page. It is a teaching tool that reinforces the silent e rule and continues to give them practice in blending.

Phonics Fundamentals II

can   can

hop   hop

Tim   Tim

rip   rip

cub   cub

fin   fin

bit   bit

tap   tap

Silent e Word Machine

1. Cut out the shapes on the dotted lines.
2. Slip the slider strip into the slits on the machine.
3. Use the word machine to show what a **silent e** can do.

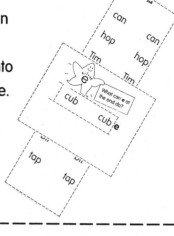

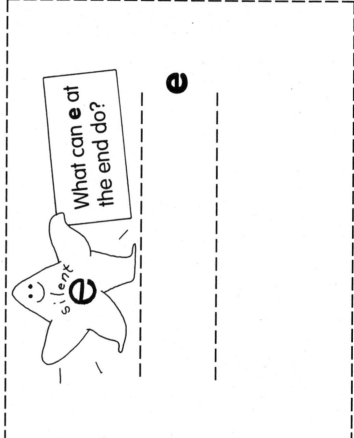

Use the machine in a variety of ways:
• Students work independently with the machine.
• You make the word with the machine and the student say them.
• You say the words and the student makes them with the machine.
• You describe or define the words and the student makes them.

Name_____

___one   ___ime   ___ope

___ive   ___ipe   ___ose

___ite   ___ate   ___ave

a b c d e f g h i j k l m n o p q r s t u v w x y z

        Phonics Fundamentals II

Name _____

___ine

___ose

___ike

___ane

___ule

___oat

___ase

___ape

___eep

a b c d e f g h i j k l m n o p q r s t u v w x y z

Phonics Fundamentals II

Name _____

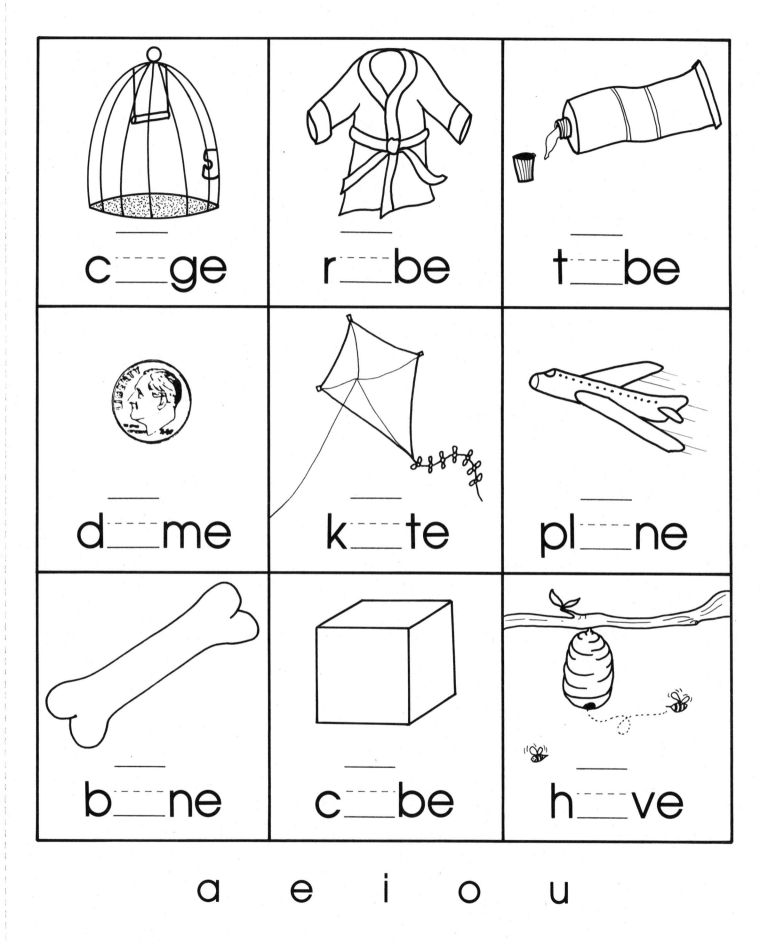

c __ ge

r __ be

t __ be

d __ me

k __ te

pl __ ne

b __ ne

c __ be

h __ ve

a   e   i   o   u

Phonics Fundamentals II

Name

m__le

c__ne

p__ne

n__se

sk__te

f__ve

m__le

c__ke

fl__te

a e i o u

Phonics Fundamentals II

Name_____

pi__e   bi__e   di__e

hi__e   roa__   goa__

cu__e   bo__e   mo__e

a b c d e f g h i j k l m n o p q r s t u v w x y z

Phonics Fundamentals II

Name____________________________

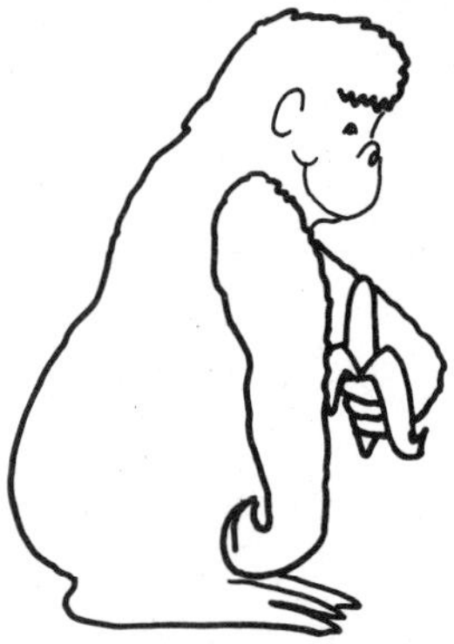 a___e	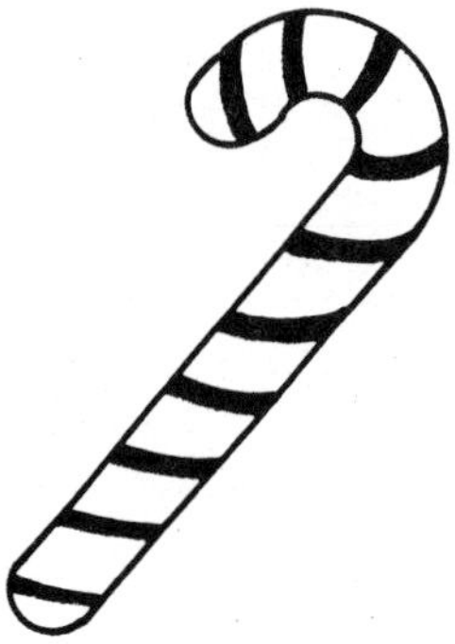 ca___e	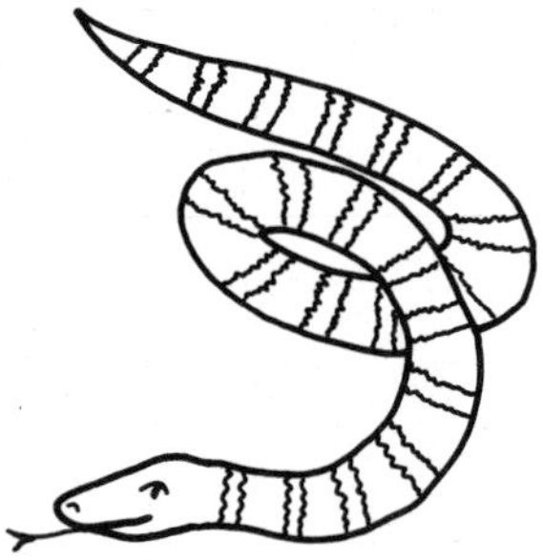 sna___e
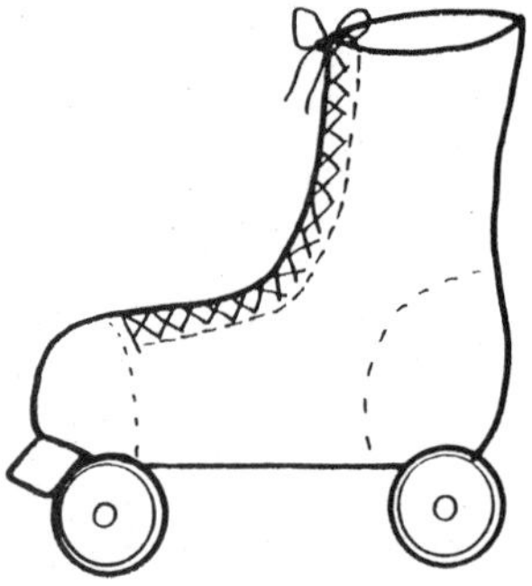 ska___e	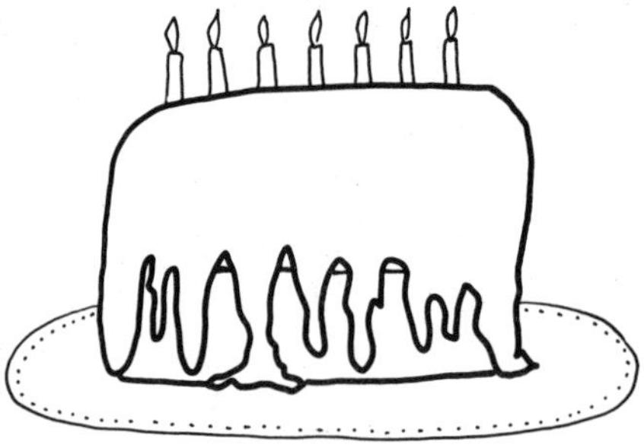 ca___e	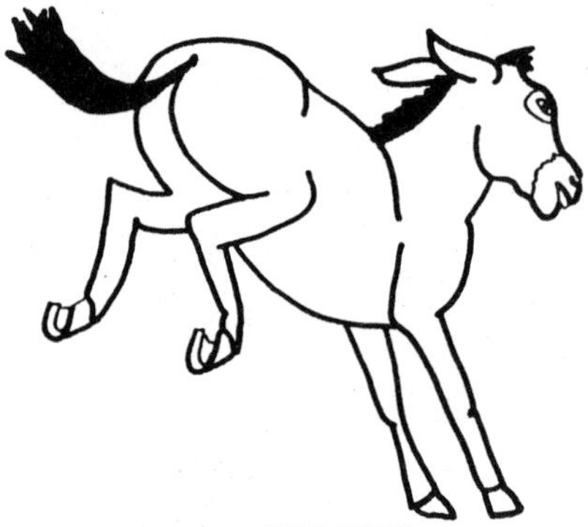 mu___e
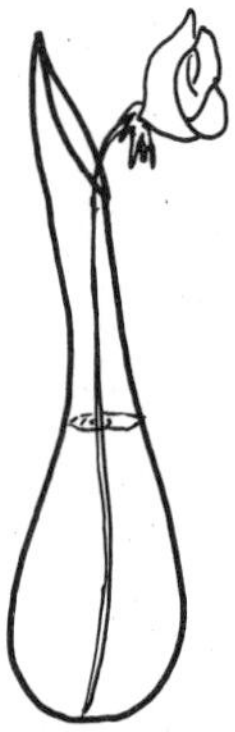 va___e	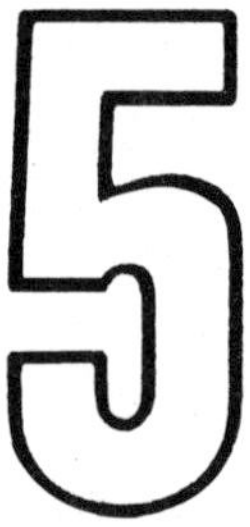 fi___e	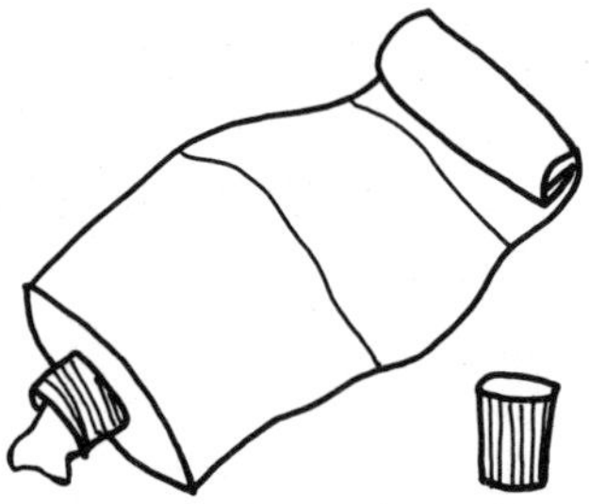 tu___e

a b c d e f g h i j k l m n o p q r s t u v w x y z

cake   rake   pine   snake

cube   nine   kite   pipe

cave   hive   ape   mule

Phonics Fundamentals II

Name _____   # Cut and paste:

bike	dime	vase	hose
mole	cage	tape	tube
robe	wave	gate	five

Name_____

Match:

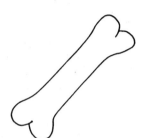

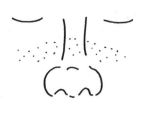

bone

kite

nine

vase

cage

nose

pipe

mole

cake

ape

Name_____

Match:

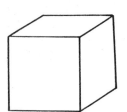

dime

gate

rose

tape

robe

bike

cube

rake

mule

five

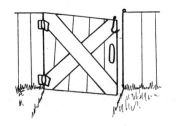

Phonics Fundamentals II

Unscramble

obne

_____

- - - - - - - - - - - -

_____

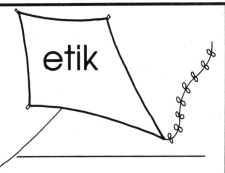

etik

_____

- - - - - - - - - - - -

_____

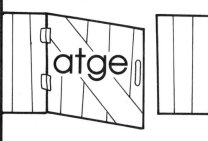

atge

_____

- - - - - - - - - - - -

_____

vefi

_____

- - - - - - - - - - - -

_____

otag

_____

- - - - - - - - - - - -

_____

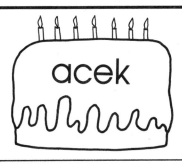

acek

_____

- - - - - - - - - - - -

_____

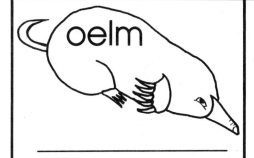

oelm

_____

- - - - - - - - - - - -

_____

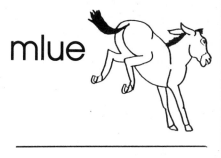

mlue

_____

- - - - - - - - - - - -

_____

meid

_____

- - - - - - - - - - - -

_____

aerk

_____

- - - - - - - - - - - -

_____

kieb

_____

- - - - - - - - - - - -

_____

avce

_____

- - - - - - - - - - - -

_____

Phonics Fundamentals II

Name _____

Name _____

Phonics Fundamentals II

Consonant Blends

**Section
Three**

Students will now be reading words that offer new challenges. They need some practice in recognizing and knowing what to do about consonant blends. These are easy to spot and easy to read. A consonant blend is nothing but a series of consonants strung together so that the sounds blend together. The sound of each letter maintains integrity but the sounds just slide into each other. These blends can appear at the beginning, middle or end of a word.

We will be practicing the following blends:

Beginning Blends		Ending Blends
glad	**br**ick	b**unk**
black	**fr**ame	fi**nd**
slip	**dr**op	la**st**
flip	**tr**ack	se**nt**
plan	**cr**ack	j**ump**
grass		

Name _____

Blends

Write the beginning sounds.

gl   pl

__ __ **ad**

gl   bl

__ __ **ack**

sl   gl

__ __ **ip**

gl   pl

My House

Kitchen Bed Bath

Livingroom Bedroom

__ __ **an**

pl   sl

__ __ **ed**

fl   gl

__ __ **ip**

Phonics Fundamentals II

Name _____

Blends

Write the beginning sounds.

dr	br
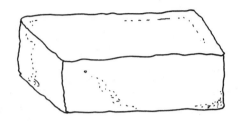
__ __ick

br	dr

__ __op

gr	tr
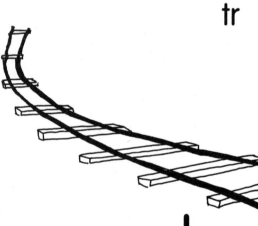
__ __ack

gr	tr

__ __apes

dr	cr

__ __ack

br	fr

__ __ame

Read and Circle

I see a bunk.
Find a black frame.

It is the last can.
I sent it back.

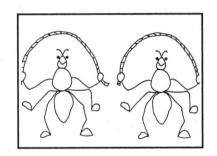

We can jump.
It is in the back.

Find the words with these blends at the end.

__ __nd   __ __st   __ __nt

__ __mp   __ __ck   __ __nk

         Phonics Fundamentals II

Name _____

He slips in the grass.

| yes | no |

front

It has a crack in the back.

| yes | no |

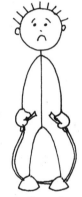

He is glad to jump.

| yes | no |

corn
bean
Soup

It is the last can.

| yes | no |

Flip it on the plate.

| yes | no |

Drop the brick in it.

| yes | no |

Vowel Combinations

ee oa ow ou oo ai ay

Now learners will discover vowel combinations; two vowels that stand together and create a common sound. We will begin by practicing the combinations **ee** and **oa**.

ee as in j**ee**p

oa as in c**oa**t

Students will practice decoding words with these combinations in the following activites. These activities continue to reinforce the short and long vowel sounds. These new combinations give the student a wider scope of phonetic skill. As he/she is exposed to new literature and written symbols in the world, you will notice a great sense of discovery as the student is able to apply what he/she learns. This is real reading!

After the student has experienced the **ee** and **oa** combination, the activity sheets continue with the introduction of five more combinations:

ow as in c**ow** ow as in **bow**	oo as in b**oo**k oo as in z**oo**
ou as in m**ou**se	ai as in p**ai**l ay as in h**ay**

Name_____

 Match:

feet

tree

bee

eel

jeep

reel

beet

seed

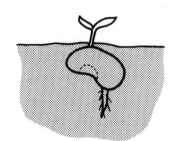

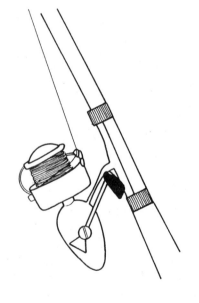

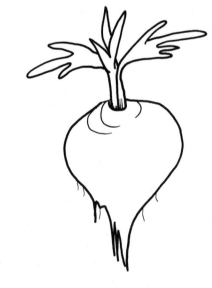

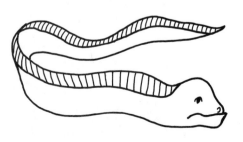

96 Phonics Fundamentals II

Name_____

Match:

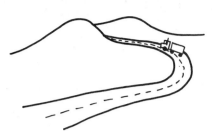

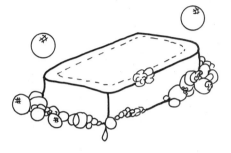

goat

toad

boat

coat

soap

road

loaf

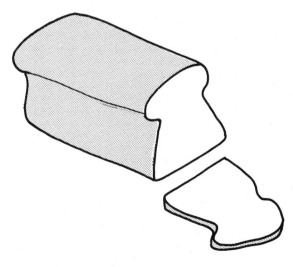

Phonics Fundamentals II

Name _____

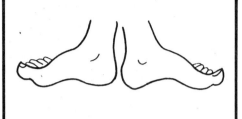

_____
- - - - - - - - - -
_____

_____
- - - - - - - - - -
_____

_____
- - - - - - - - - -
_____

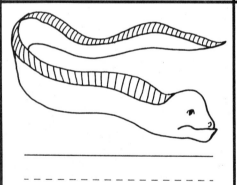

_____
- - - - - - - - - -
_____

_____
- - - - - - - - - -
_____

_____
- - - - - - - - - -
_____

_____
- - - - - - - - - -
_____

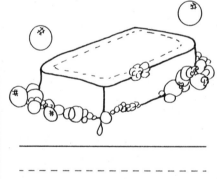

_____
- - - - - - - - - -
_____

_____
- - - - - - - - - -
_____

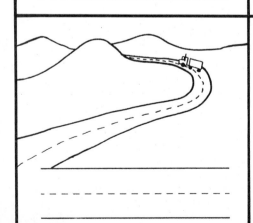

_____
- - - - - - - - - -
_____

_____
- - - - - - - - - -
_____

_____
- - - - - - - - - -
_____

Name _____

Match:

a bone on the plate

a kite in a tree

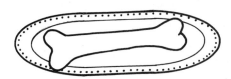

a bike on the road

a snake in a cage

a toad in a hole

a goat in a jeep

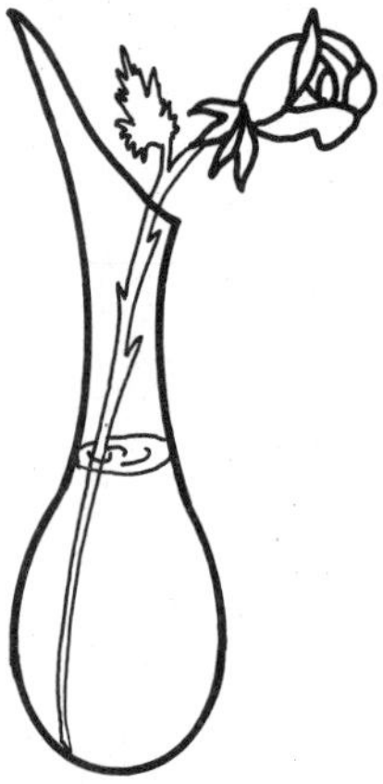

a_____ in a_____

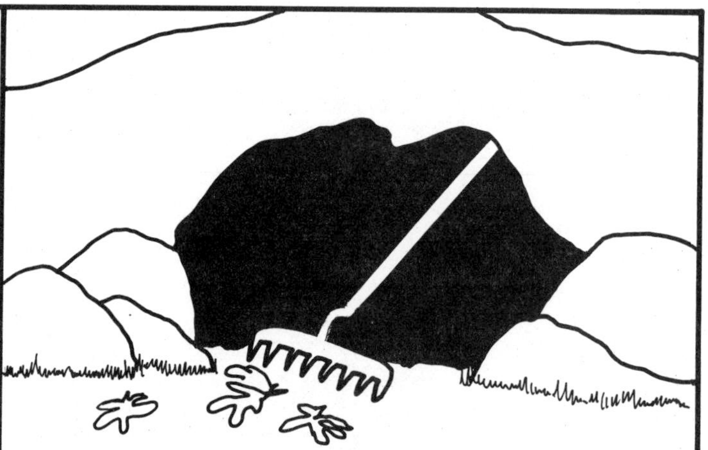

a_____ in a_____

a_____ on a_____

a_____ in the_____

an_____ on a_____

a_____ in a_____

Name_____

Match:

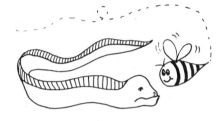

a robe and a coat

a goat and a mule

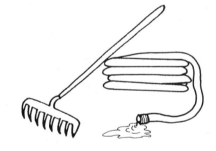

a rose and a vine

an eel and a bee

a rake and a hose

a kite and a bike

Name_____ Read and color:

1. Make the bee hive brown.
2. Make nine bees yellow.
3. Make five bees black.
4. Make the vine green.
5. Make the snake red and black.
6. Make the rake orange.

   Phonics Fundamentals II

Name_____

Read and draw:

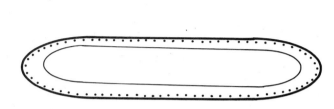

a big cake on the
blue plate

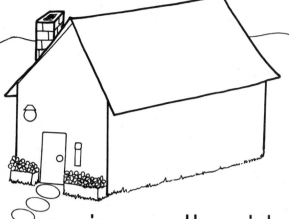

a vine on the side
of the home

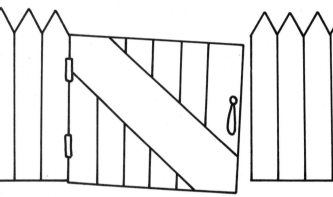

a snake on the
brown gate

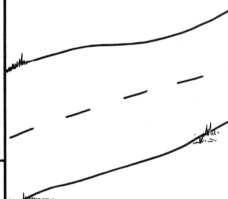

a toad in the road

a kite up in the tree

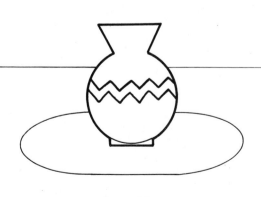

a rose in the vase

Phonics Fundamentals II

Name_____

Match:

Pete rode his bike.

Will Jake bite the bone?

The mule was by the hole.

Dave broke the vase.

A note is on the tree.

Put the hose by the rose.

Phonics Fundamentals II

Name_____

Match:

The dime fell in a hole.

Kate's cake is on the plate.

The cane is by his cape.

A name is on that line.

Pete can drive the jeep.

June's boat is on the lake.

       Phonics Fundamentals II

Name_____

Cut and paste:

A goat ate the cake.	See Dave dive into the lake.
Jane had a flute.	Zeke ate beets for lunch.
He rode in the plane.	A pine tree is by the road.

Name_____ Read and answer:

yes   no

1. Did the snake hide in the cave? _____

2. Did Kate ride up the hill? _____

3. Did Kate and Pete meet at the top? _____

4. Is it a hot day? _____

5. Did Pete hike up the hill? _____

6. Can a snake ride a bike? _____

         Phonics Fundamentals II

Name_____

1. A _____ sat in the jeep.

2. The _____ has on a coat.

3. The toad has a _____ .

4. The goat can ride a _____ .

5. A _____ is on skates.

6. A snake is under the _____ .

bike
goat
jeep
kite
mole
mule

108   Phonics Fundamentals II

Scrambled Sentence Fun

1.   woke   Lee   late.   up

_____

- -

_____

_____

- -

_____

2.   Will   Mike   lake?   the   like

_____

- -

_____

_____

- -

_____

3.   went   a   Jake   for   hike.

_____

- -

_____

_____

- -

_____

4.   Zeke   Did   take   big   of   cake?   a   bite

_____

- -

_____

_____

- -

_____

Name_____

Read and draw:

Put a green coat and hat
on Gene.

Make three bees
by the hive.

Make skates on Jane's feet.

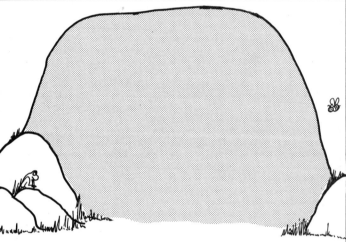

Put five bats in the cave.

Make nine trees
on the steep hill.

Make the cake brown
and the rose yellow.

 Phonics Fundamentals II

Name_____ Read and answer:

yes   no

_____

1. Is a bone on a plate?

_____

2. Did Dave ride his bike?

_____

3. Can you see five cupcakes?

_____

4. Can Dave and Eve see the
   snake on the tree?

_____

5. Did the dog bite the bone?

_____

6. Did Eve hide in back of the tree?_____

 Phonics Fundamentals II

Name_____   # Read and color:

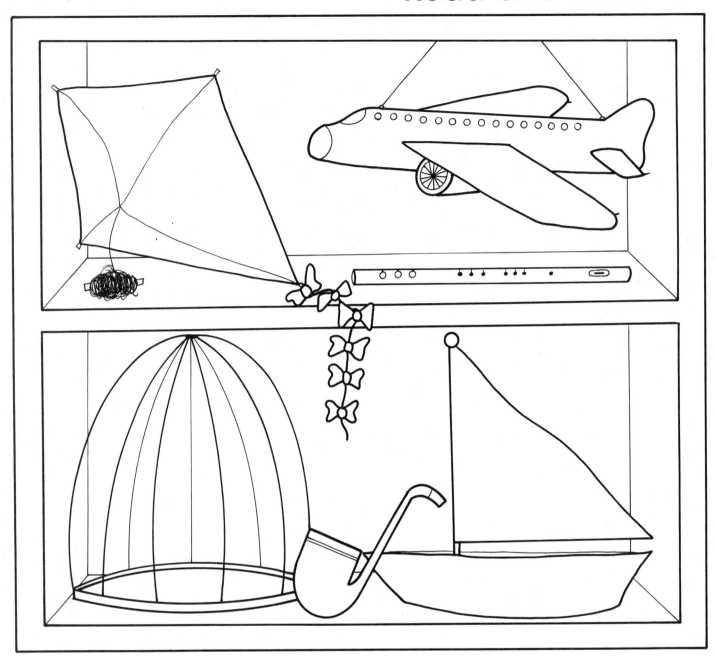

1. Make the flute brown.
2. Put a yellow sun on the boat.
3. Put five green spots on the kite.
4. Make an ape in the cage.
5. Put a name on the side of the plane.
6. Make the pipe purple.

                   Phonics Fundamentals II

Name _____ **Read and color:**

1. Make a blue boat in Pete's box.
2. Put nine candles on Mike's cake.
3. Put an orange and green kite in Lee's box.
4. Make Zeke's boat yellow.
5. Put socks for Mike in Kate's box.
6. A brown ape is in June's box.
   Make the ape's cape red.

Phonics Fundamentals II

Name_____

Write:

1. it a the cave? Is mile to

_____

- -

_____

- -

2. at the tree. me Meet pine

_____

- -

_____

- -

3. Mike note see the Did on gate? the

_____

- -

_____

- -

4. Eve's fell kite the into tree.

_____

- -

_____

- -

Note: Cut the puzzle pieces apart. Scramble the pieces and then try to match the words and pictures.

Puzzle

rain

pail

hay

mouse

cow

book

bow

zoo

Name _____

ai as in r**ai**n
ay as in pl**ay**

Rain, rain go away,

Come again another day.

Little _____ likes to play.
_{name}

Write words here:

ai	ay
_____	_____
_____	_____
_____	_____
_____	_____
	_____

Name _____

Surprise!

ow as in c**ow**

paste

paste

paste

ow as in b**ow**

paste

paste

paste

row

sow

plow

pow

mow

tow

117

Phonics Funcamentals II

Name _____

b**oo**k

paste

paste

paste

z**oo**

paste

paste

paste

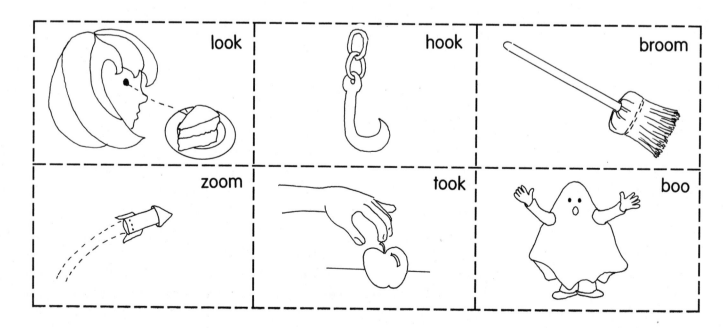

look

hook

broom

zoom

took

boo

Name _____

OW	OO	OU

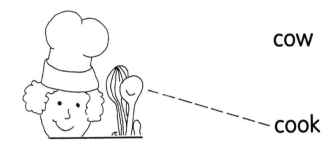

cow

cook

hoop

house

bow

book

boo

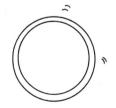

hook

spout

Name _____   Finish the sentence.

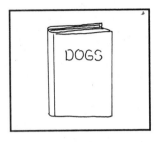

I see a red _____ .
book   look

I ran _____ the _____ .
down   frown   road   toad

Get the green_____.
pail   rain

The _____ is on the man.
bow   blow

It is not a big _____ .
mouse   house

Name _____

| ai | ay | ow | oo | ou |

Circle the correct picture.

The hay is in the box.

I see a book in a nook.

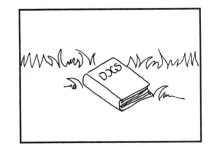

I can see the rain.

The cook is sad.

The house is in the rain.

Consonant Surprises

Section Five

sh th ch wh

Sometimes consonants sit together to make completely new sounds. Let's share with our students what **sh, th, ch** and **wh** can do. These sounds are distinguished by specific mouth and tongue positions. It helps students remember these combinations if they can make the following associations:

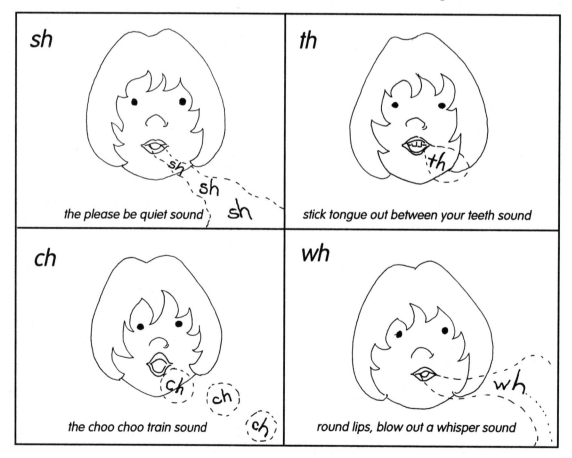

sh — the please be quiet sound

th — stick tongue out between your teeth sound

ch — the choo choo train sound

wh — round lips, blow out a whisper sound

The activities in this chapter give students an opportunity to listen for these consonant combinations at the beginning of words. Students will soon be hearing and reading them anywhere they find them.

Name _____

th ~~**sh**~~

30

Name _____

ch

wh

Name _____

wh sh ch th

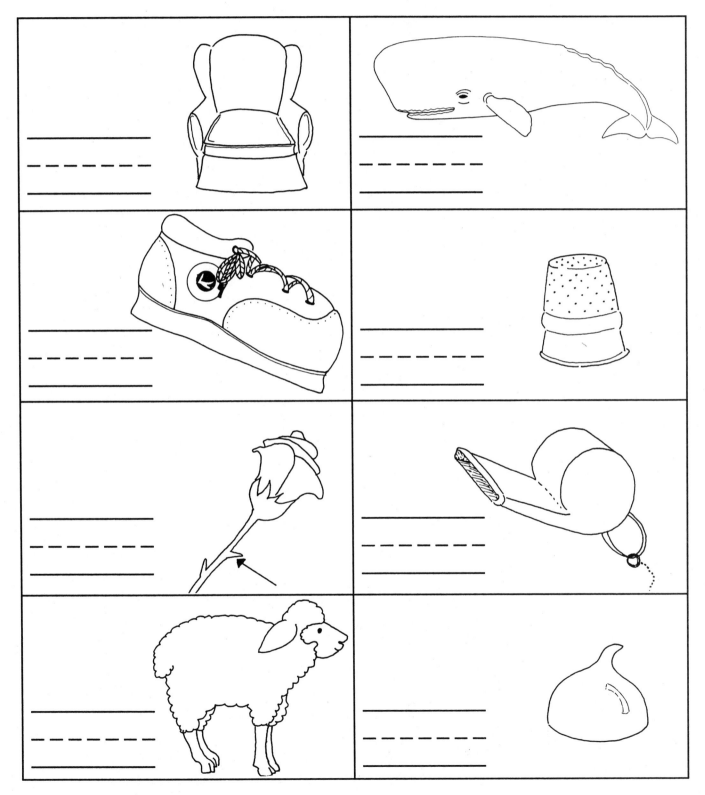

Name _____

wh sh ch th

_____
- - - - - - -
_____

_____
- - - - - - -
_____

_____
- - - - - - -
_____

_____
- - - - - - -
_____

_____
- - - - - - -
_____

_____
- - - - - - -
_____

_____
- - - - - - -
_____

_____
- - - - - - -
_____

Phonics Fundamentals II

Game

Can you match the picture to the beginning sound?
Each box must have the same number of cards.

th

Put the cards here.

sh

Put the cards here.

ch

Put the cards here.

wh

Put the cards here.

Phonics Fundamentals II

Use with page 127.

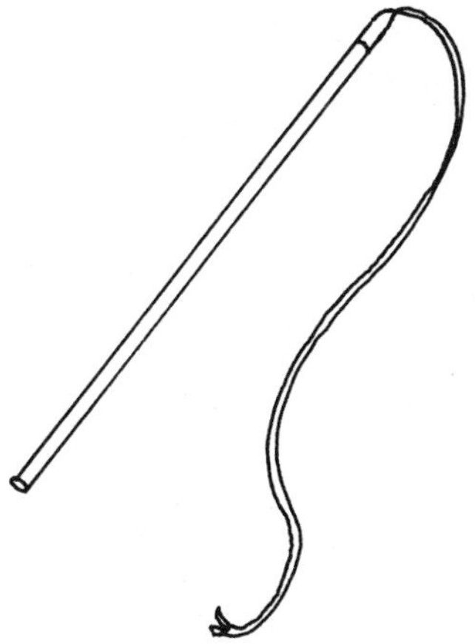

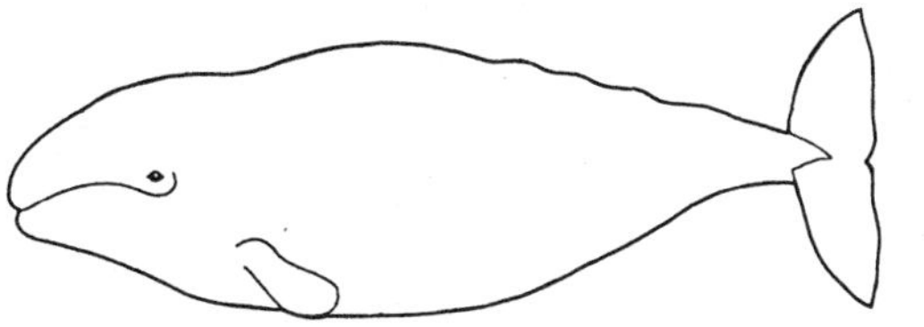

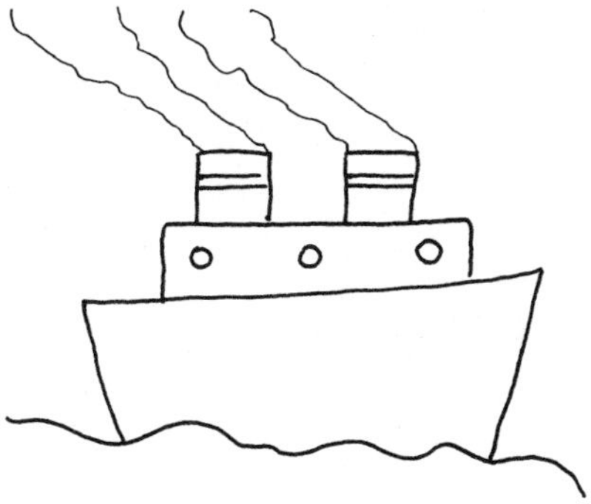

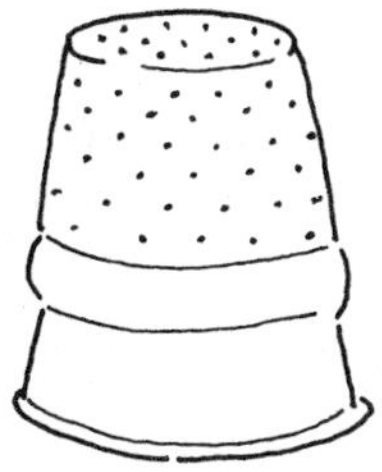

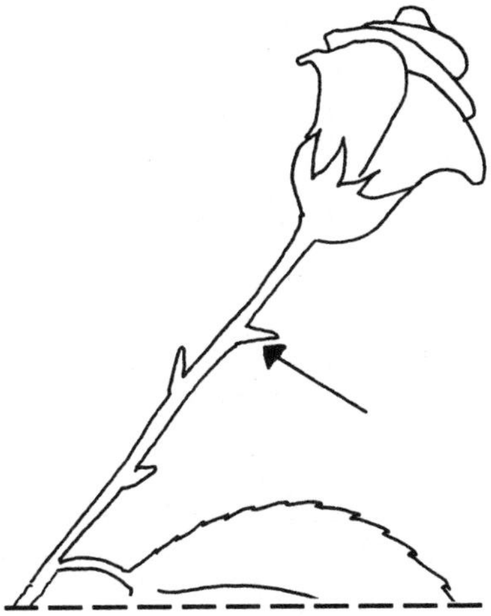

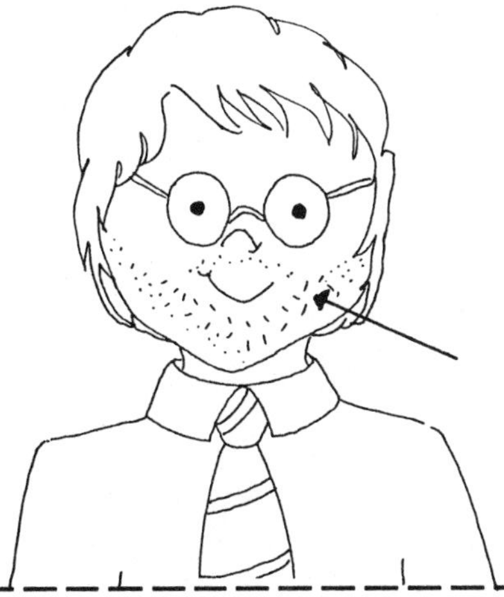

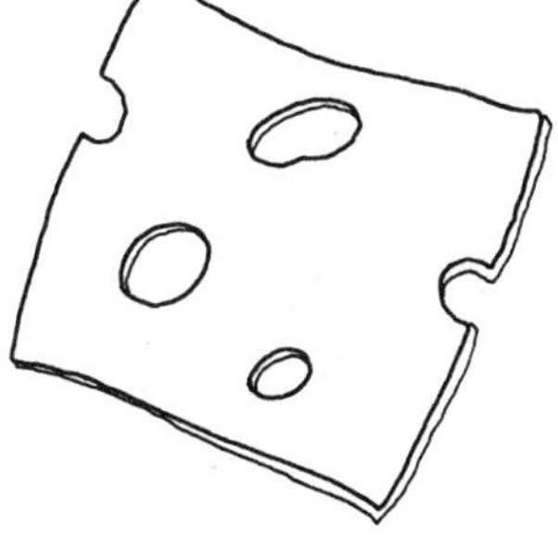

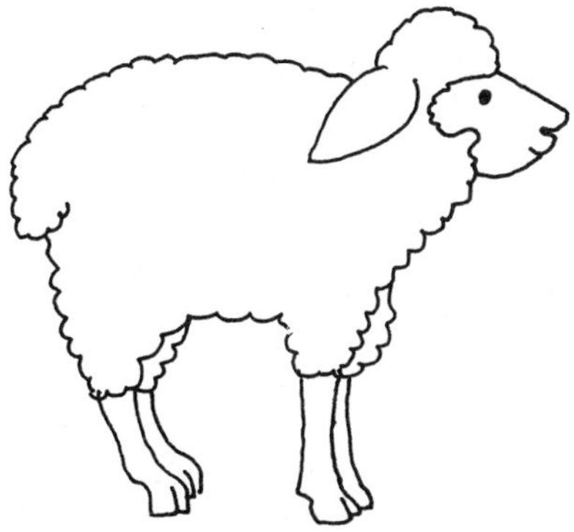

Rhyming Words

Section Six

Learning to recognize rhyming words is a rich discovery for a beginning reader. The rhyming words make reading fun and allow the student to greatly increase his or her reading vocabulary.

By teaching the concept of rhyming words, you are also introducing the concept of word families. Students will now see how it is possible to create many new words by changing the initial sound. *Get* becomes *met, wet, set* and *pet*. Students will begin seeing word families everywhere.

can	but	bit	bug
pan	cut	fit	jug
ran	nut	hit	hug
man	hut	sit	rug
plan	shut	flit	plug

Listening to poems, nursery rhymes and songs also strengthens the student's ability to listen for rhyming words. Share literature and poetry daily with your students to reinforce this appreciation for language and rhyme.

Let students use the puzzles on the following pages to practice listening for rhyming words.

Rhyming Puzzles

wink	sink	mouse	house
star	jar	shell	bell
lock	clock	honey	money
dove	glove	plane	train
bee	knee	pear	stair

131

Phonics Fundamentals II

Rhyming Puzzles

frog	log
van	fan
bat	hat
sun	bun
jam	ram
bed	sled
fox	box
hen	pen
crown	clown
boat	goat

Phonics Fundamentals II

Phonics Fundamentals II

Name_____

Circle the pictures that rhyme.

1.

2.

3. 10

4.

5.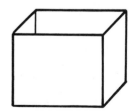

Name_____

Color the pictures that rhyme with:

red

blue

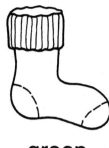
green

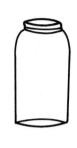
yellow

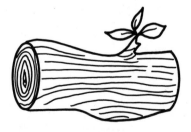

Name _____

Circle the words that rhyme.

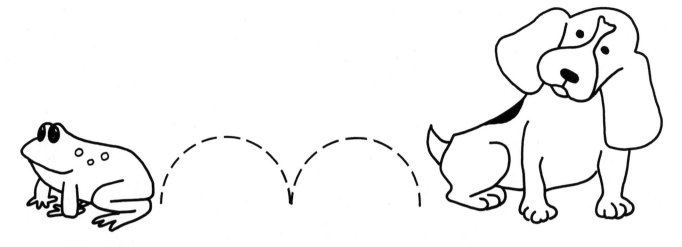

1.	bug	rug	bun	hug
2.	bell	ball	tell	well
3.	map	mop	hop	top
4.	dog	log	box	hog
5.	in	can	pin	fin
6.	nut	sun	hut	cut

Phonics Fundamentals II

Name_____

Finish the words.

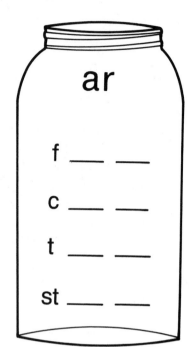

ar

f _ _ _

c _ _ _

t _ _ _

st _ _ _

en

h _ _ _

t _ _ _

p _ _ _

m _ _ _

ig

p _ _ _

d _ _ _

b _ _ _

w _ _ _

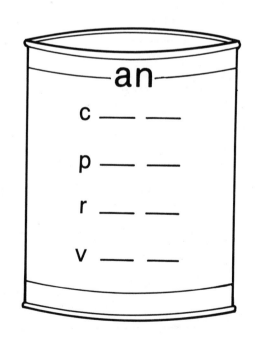

an

c _ _ _

p _ _ _

r _ _ _

v _ _ _

138

Phonics Fundamentals II

Name_____

Cut and paste the pictures that rhyme.

Phonics Fundamentals II

Name _____

Add one letter to name the picture.

___an   ___an   ___an

___en   ___en   ___en

___ig   ___ig   ___ig

Phonics Fundamentals II

Name _____

Color the words that rhyme with **at**.

bug	can	dog	den / pat	let
big / bat	hop / fat	jam / hat	slat	fun / cat
mat / vat	splat	Nat	at ●	that
sat / met	Pat / fox	flat / get	brat	rat / nap
pot	win	man	tat / run	bed

I see a _____.

Name _____

Fill in the missing words.

1. It is _____ to _____ in the _____ .

sun	fun	run

2. _____ put grape _____ on his _____ .

ham	jam	Sam

3. _____ has a big _____ _____ .

red	Fred	sled

4. Can a _____ _____ in a _____ ?

boat	goat	float

Phonics Fundamentals II

Name _____

Match the pictures that rhyme.

Name _____

Circle the words that rhyme.
Draw a line to the picture.

1. A (fat)(cat)(sat)
   on (that)(hat.)

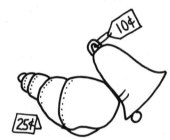

2. Dan can ride
   in his tan van.

3. Get the wet pet
   out of the net.

4. I wish I had
   a fish in a dish.

5. Did you sell the
   shell and the bell?

       Phonics Fundamentals II

Name _____

Write the rhyming word.

| log | wig | pen | box | vet |

1. See the fox in that _____ .

2. A green frog sat on the _____ .

3. Can a pig put on a _____ ?

4. I took my pet to see the _____ .

5. Put the hen in her _____ .

 Phonics Fundamentals II

Mark the words that rhyme.

hog   oat

Name _____

Match the words that rhyme.

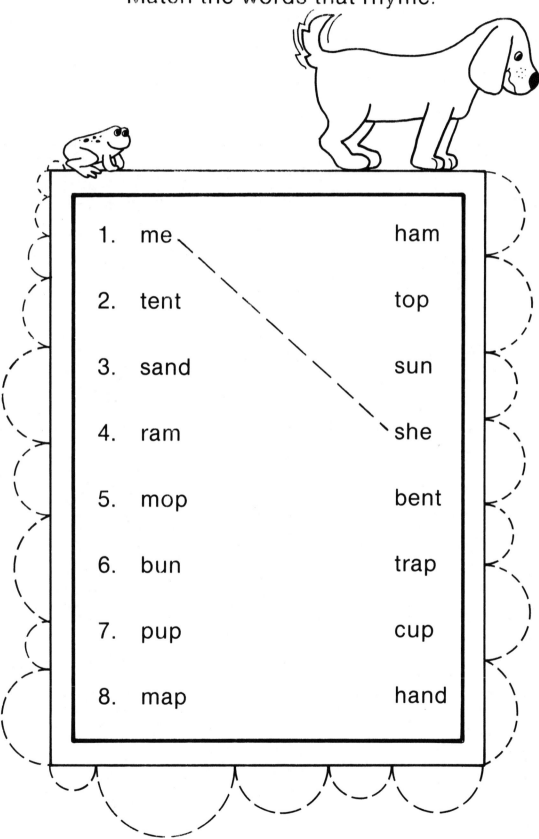

1.	me		ham
2.	tent		top
3.	sand		sun
4.	ram		she
5.	mop		bent
6.	bun		trap
7.	pup		cup
8.	map		hand

Name _____

Circle the rhyming words.
Color the picture.

a green (bug)
on a black (rug)

a red hen
in a brown pen

an orange ball
on a tall wall

a yellow fish
in a blue dish

Phonics Fundamentals II

Name _____

Write the rhyming words.

pink	make	wink
deep	keep	peep
rake	sleep	flake
weep	take	think
shake	sink	drink

cake

ink

keep

1._____

2._____

3._____

4._____

5._____

1._____

2._____

3._____

4._____

5._____

1._____

2._____

3._____

4._____

5._____

 Phonics Fundamentals II

Name_____

Color the words that rhyme.

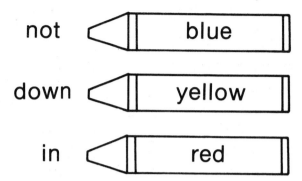

not ◁ blue

down ◁ yellow

in ◁ red

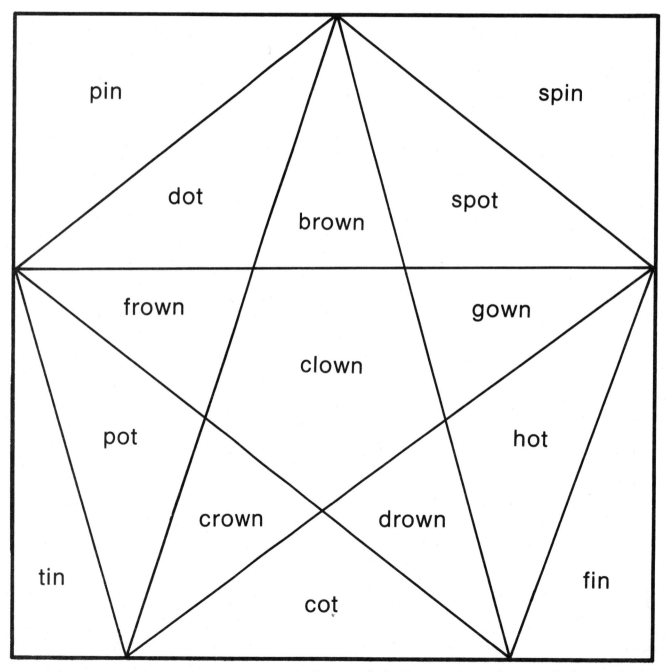

pin

spin

dot

spot

brown

frown

gown

clown

pot

hot

tin

crown

drown

fin

cot

Name_____

Color the pictures that rhyme.

Finish the word families.

ell

sh ___ ___ ___

f ___ ___ ___

sp ___ ___ ___

w ___ ___ ___

t ___ ___ ___

ent

t ___ ___ ___

r ___ ___ ___

b ___ ___ ___

d ___ ___ ___

s ___ ___ ___

ook

b ___ ___ ___

l ___ ___ ___

cr ___ ___ ___

sh ___ ___ ___

br ___ ___ ___

ail

p ___ ___ ___

m ___ ___ ___

t ___ ___ ___

tr ___ ___ ___

qu ___ ___ ___

Read the words to a friend.

Name _____

Riddle Rhymes

Draw

1. I am a fat hog.

_____   _____
- - - - - - - - - - - - -   - - - - - - - - - - - - -
_____   _____

2. I am a brown pot.

_____   _____
- - - - - - - - - - - - -   - - - - - - - - - - - - -
_____   _____

3. I am a silly rabbit.

_____   _____
- - - - - - - - - - - - -   - - - - - - - - - - - - -
_____   _____

4. I am a home for guppies.

_____   _____
- - - - - - - - - - - - -   - - - - - - - - - - - - -
_____   _____

| bunny | dish | big | fish |
| tan | pig | pan | funny |

 Phonics Fundamentals II

Name ______________________________

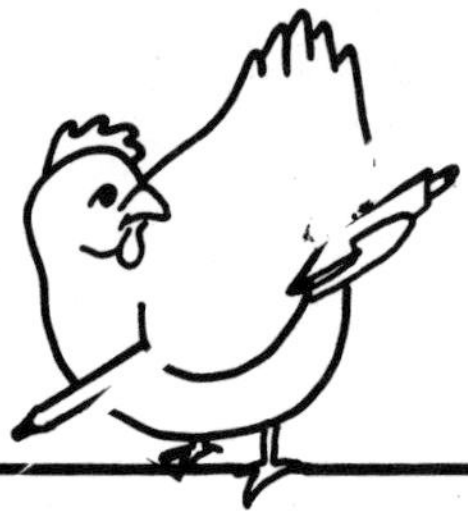

Circle the words that rhyme.

Draw the picture.

a hot pot on a red spot	a brown clown falling down
a bent tent with a dent	a clean green bean

Name_____

Write some words that rhyme.

it	an	pot
1._____	1._____	1._____
2._____	2._____	2._____
3._____	3._____	3._____

me	bun	get
1._____	1._____	1._____
2._____	2._____	2._____
3._____	3._____	3._____

Name _____

Match the pictures that rhyme.

ghost

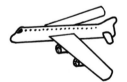

rain

pail

chair

 Phonics Fundamentals II

Name _____

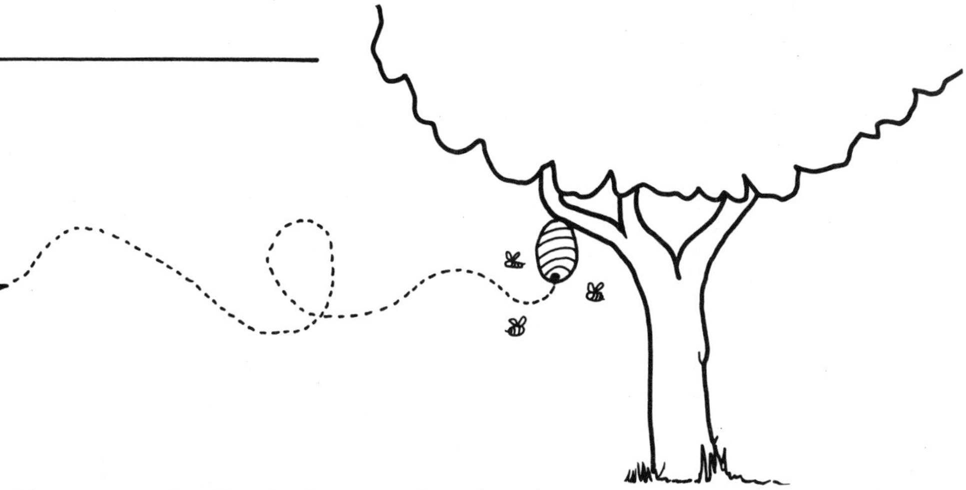

Write the words that rhyme in the boxes.

see	rain	zoo

three   shoe

plane   too

chain   pea

you   blue

bee   train

Name _____

Follow the words that rhyme with <u>take</u> to get to the <u>cake</u>.

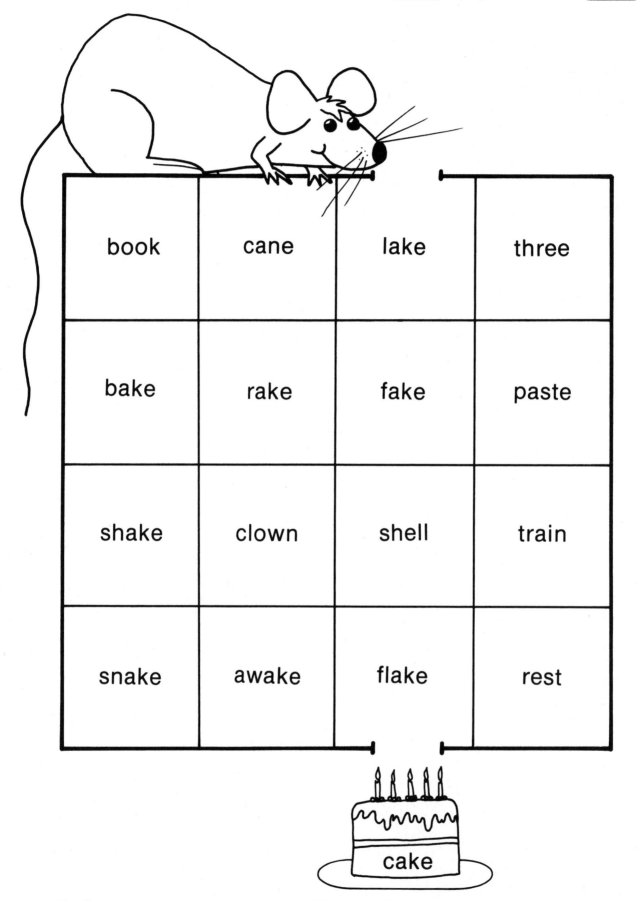

book	cane	lake	three
bake	rake	fake	paste
shake	clown	shell	train
snake	awake	flake	rest

cake

Phonics Fundamentals II

Name _____

Paste the rhyming words by the pictures.

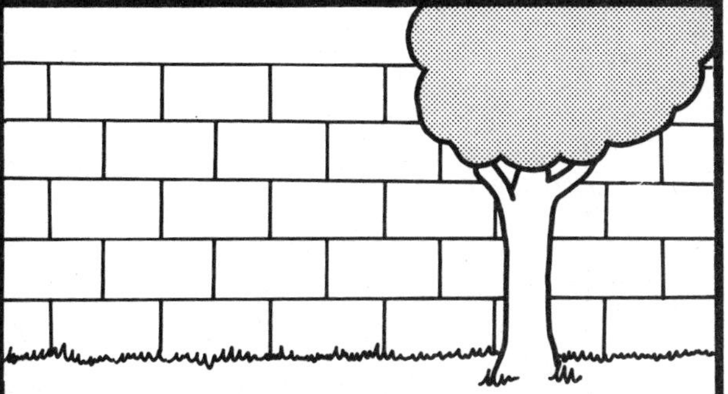

quail trail	tall wall	wet pet
clown frown	mouse house	pig wig

Name_____

Write some words that rhyme.

cake	well	down

sock	ink	all

Phonics Fundamentals II

Name_____   Write the rhyming words.

| dock | hill | Muffet | clock | sheep |
| day | Peep | away | tuffet | Jill |

1. Jack and _____

Went up the _____.

2. Little Bo _____

Has lost her _____.

3. Hickory, dickory, _____

The mouse ran up the _____.

4. Little Miss _____

Sat on a _____.

5. Rain, rain go _____

Come again another _____.

Name_____

Circle the words that rhyme.
Draw a line to the picture.

1. A (mouse) ran into
   the dog (house.)

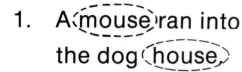

2. I think the pink drink
   is by the sink.

3. Do you have a new
   blue shoe?

4. Her pail is for sale at
   the end of the trail.

5. A dragon sat on
   my wagon.

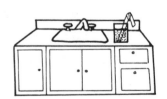

6. I love the dove
   on my glove.

162   Phonics Fundamentals II

Name_____

Color the words that rhyme with:

funny 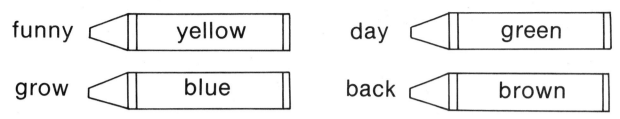 yellow   day   green

grow   blue   back   brown

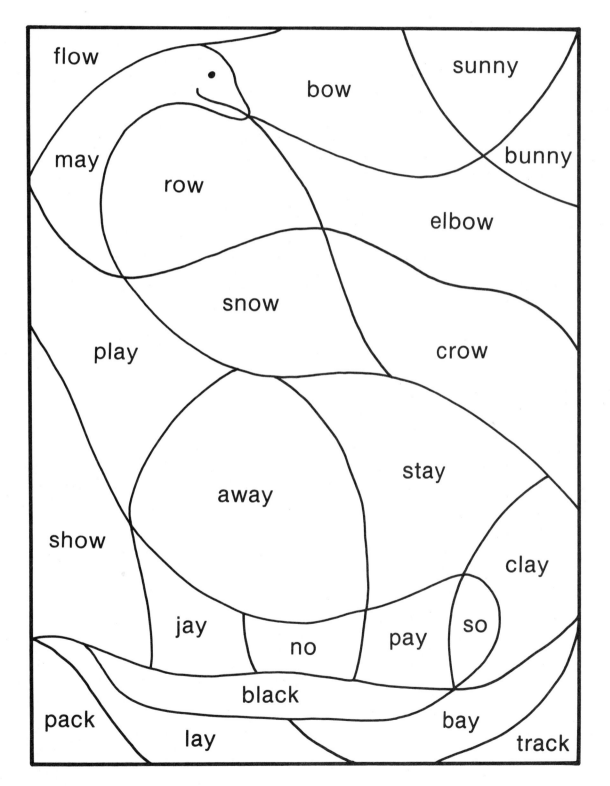

flow

sunny

bow

may

bunny

row

elbow

snow

play

crow

stay

away

show

clay

jay

so

no   pay

black

pack

bay

lay

track

Simple Short Vowel Stories
Individual Student Books

Section Seven

These twelve stories about Bob and his pet dog Sam give children the practice they need in reading simple short vowel words. They are a strong addition to any reading program because they offer children their very own copy of a book they can actually read and take home to share with their parents. Most words contain short vowels and are single syllable.

There are a few words that will need to be taught by sight. The practice word cards in this chapter are provided to introduce this sight vocabulary. Children may use these cards for practice at school or at home. A pattern for an envelope in which to keep the cards is also included.

The Word List		
a	go	to
for	do	we
see	the	he
shop	paw	tail
bath	trick	bone

There are stories with four pages, six pages, and eight pages. All of the stories are about the adventures of an older man named Bob and his pet dog, Sam. Bob is a kind man who loves Sam in spite of his mischievous ways.

How to put the books together:

1. Remove the pages for each story from the book.
Reproduce the pages to create a copy for each child .

2. Cut on the dotted lines. Put the pages in sequence and staple them together. The books are ready to read!

Phonics Fundamentals II

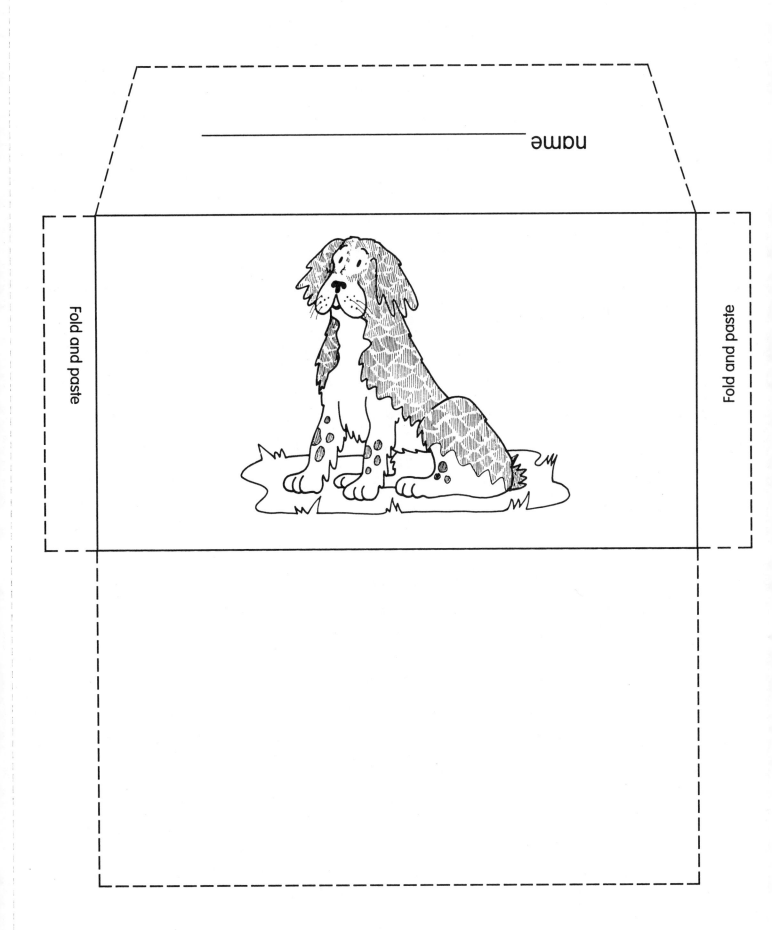

name _____

Fold and paste

Fold and paste

a	trick	shop
see	to	do
bath	he	paw
go	bone	we
the	for	tail

Phonics Fundamentals II

Sam

Sam is a dog.

Sam can wag.
Wag, Sam, wag.

Sam can run.
Run fast Sam.

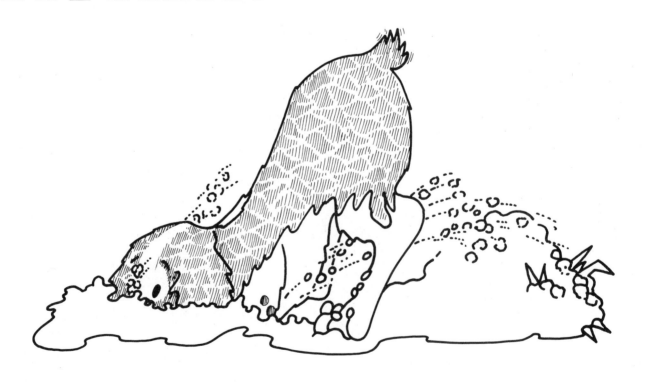

Sam can dig.
Bad dog, Sam.

Bob

Bob has a shop.
It is a fix-it shop.

1

Can Bob fix it?
Can Bob fix the dent?

3

A box is in the shop.
The box has a dent.

Bob did fix the box.

Bob and Sam

Bob has a pet.
The pet is Sam.
Bob went up the hill.
Sam went up the hill.

1

Run, Sam, run.
Get the hat.
Will Sam get the hat?

3

Bob had a hat.
The hat fell.

Sam got the hat.
Bob pets Sam.

The Van

Bob has a van.
The van is big and red.

The van can go up a hill.
The van can go fast.

Get in the van, Bob.
Get in the van, Sam.

2 The Van

Go, Bob. Go, Sam.
It is fun to go in the van.

4 The Van

At the Pond

The pond is big.
A log is in the pond.
A frog is on the log. ____

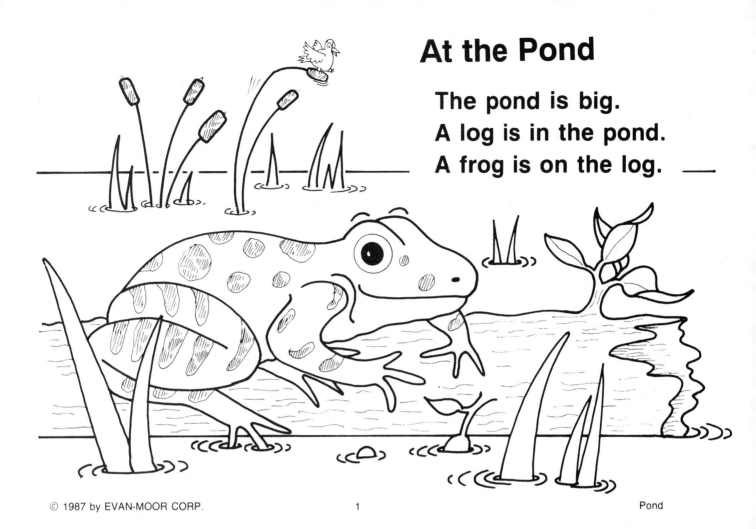

1 Pond

Sam runs to the pond.
Sam can see the frog.
Can Sam get the frog?

3 Pond

The frog can see a bug.
Can the frog get the bug?
It did get the bug.

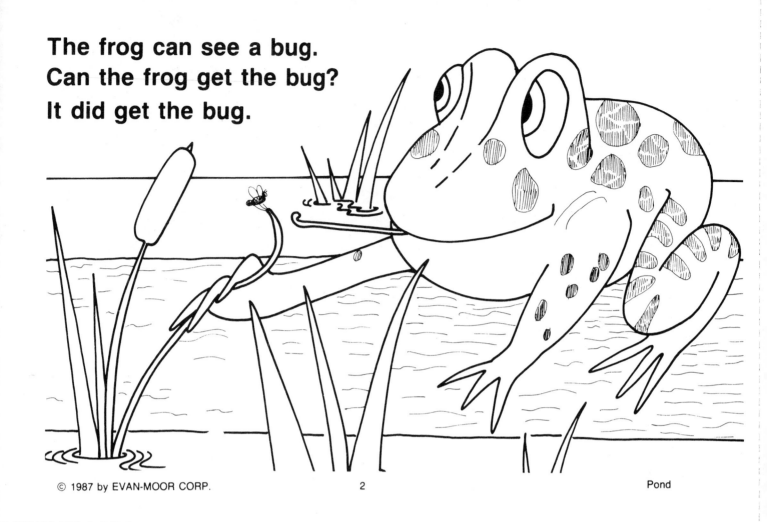

2 Pond

Sam did not get the frog.
Sam got wet!
Sam is a mess.

4 Pond

A Bone for Sam

1 Bone

Sam runs to Bob.
Will Sam get the bone?

3 Bone

Bob sits on the step.
Bob has a bone.

2 Bone

Sit, Sam, sit.
Sam must sit to get the bone.

4 Bone

Bob set the bone on Sam's paw.
Sit, Sam, sit.
Do not get the bone.

5

Bone

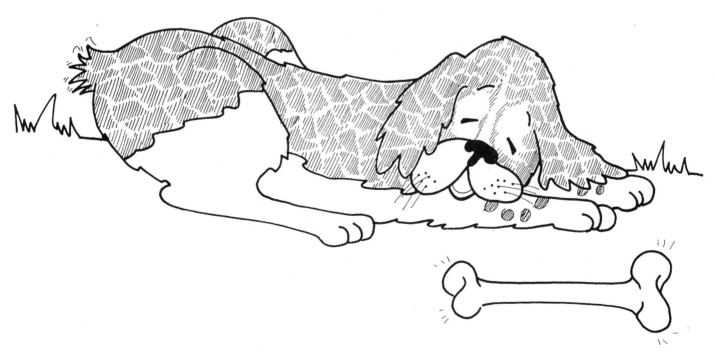

Sam is glad.
He has the bone.

7

Bone

Get the bone, Sam.
Sam gets the bone.
Sam wags his tail.

The End

Bob Helps

Les had to land.
He will get Bob to help.

1   Les

Get in, Bob.
We can go up.

Stop, Sam.
Do not get in.

3   Les

Bob and Sam go to the pond.
Bob can help.
He did fix it.

2 Les

Sam is sad.
He can not go.

Bob is glad.
He can go up, up, up.

4 Les

The Bath

Sam ran and ran.
He got wet.

1 Bath

Pam sees Sam in the mud.
Pam runs to get Bob.

3 Bath

Sam dug in the mud.
He had fun.

2

Bath

Sam is a mess.
He must get a bath.

4

Bath

Bob got a tub.
Pam got a rag.
Get in the tub, Sam.

5 Bath

Bob ran fast.
Bob got Sam.

7 Bath

Sam did not get in the tub.
Sam ran and ran.

6 Bath

Sam is in the tub.
Sam will not be a mess.

8 Bath

Camp

It is hot in the shop.
We can go in the van.
We can camp.

1 Camp

Bob set the tent on the sand.
Bob set the box in the tent.

3 Camp

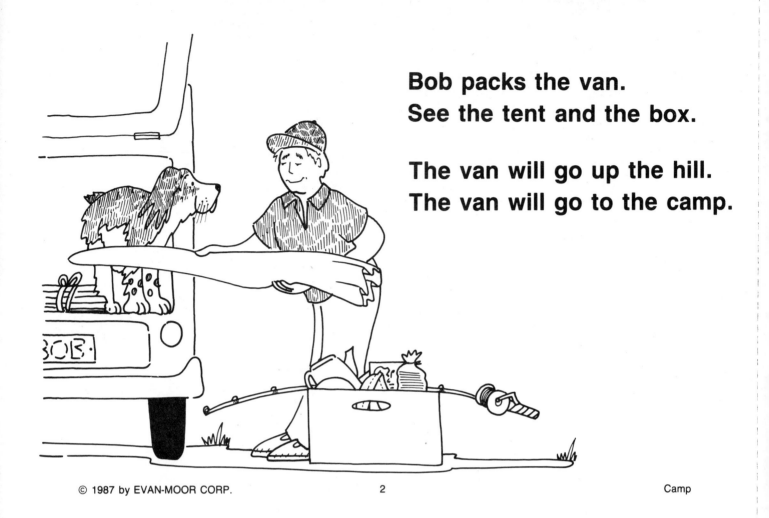

Bob packs the van.
See the tent and the box.

The van will go up the hill.
The van will go to the camp.

2 Camp

Bob and Sam run on the sand.
It is fun to camp.

4 Camp

Pam's Pet

Bob and Sam went to see Pam.
Bob had a box.
The box had a lid.

1

Pam

Get the lid, Pam.

3

Pam

Bob set the box on the step.

Pam sees the box.

Pam can not see in it.

2   Pam

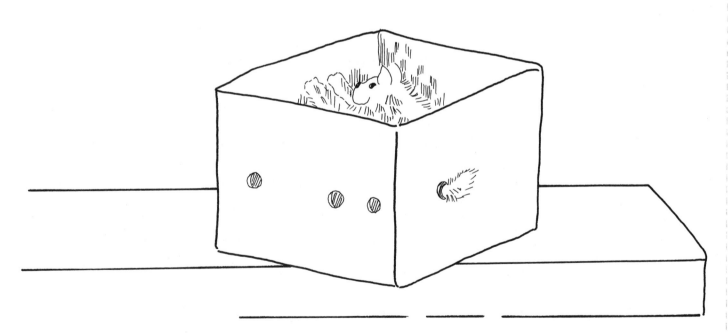

Gus is in the box.

Gus is a cat.

He is not a big cat.

4   Pam

Gus is a pet for Pam.
Pam pets Gus.
Pam is glad.

Pam

Pam and Gus sit on the step.

Pam

Bob and Sam must go.
Pam hugs Bob.
Pam hugs Sam.

6 Pam

A pet cat is fun.

8 Pam

Sam's Trick

Bob and Sam go up the hill.
Bob has a stick.
He will toss the stick.

1   Sam's Trick

Sam got the stick.
He ran back to Bob.

3   Sam's Trick

Run, Sam, run.
Run up the hill.
Get the stick.

2

Sam's Trick

Sam sees a box.
He runs to the box.

4

Sam's Trick

Sam is stuck in the box.
Sam is sad.
He must get help.

5 Sam's Trick

The box is off Sam.
Sam is glad.

7 Sam's Trick

Bob helps Sam.
He gets the box off Sam
Bob pets Sam.
Sam licks Bob.

6

Run, Sam, run.

8

Sam and Gus

Pam has a pig.
The pig can not go.
Pam must go to the fix-it shop.

Gus sees Sam on the step.
Gus runs to Sam.
Gus and Sam go up the hill.

Pam went to see Bob.
Gus went to see Sam.

2 Pig

Bob can fix the pig.
He will fix it for Pam.
Pam can help Bob.

4 Pig

Pam had to go.
Pam got the pig.
Pam went to get Gus.

5

Pig

Bob went up the hill.
He did not see the pets.

7

Pig

Pam did not see Gus and Sam.
Pam went to get Bob.
Can Bob get the pets?

6

Pig

Bob went to the pond.
He did see the pets.
See Sam and Gus on the log.

Pam, Gus, and the pig can go.

8

Pig

Simple Long Vowel Stories
Individual Student Books

Section Eight

These nine stories about Zeke, his friends, and their adventures give children the practice they need in reading simple long vowel words. The stories can be used in the classroom or sent home to be read to parents.

Most of the stories contain short vowel or simple long vowel words. There are silent e words and some vowel blends have been used. There are also words that will need to be taught by sight. The following pages contain word cards and an envelope pattern. Select the words you feel your students need to practice.

The Word List

are	do	friends	look	put	this	where
Aunt	down	from	my	said	tire	yelled
ball	eat	funny	next	saw	to	you
been	faster	girls	oh	school	too	yard
boys	find	have	park	start	twins	
come	fire	her	party	than	them	
dirt	for	live	play	the		

How to put the books together:

1. Remove the pages for each story from the book.
Reproduce the pages to create a copy for each child .

2. Cut on the dotted lines. Put the pages in sequence and staple them together. The books are ready to read!

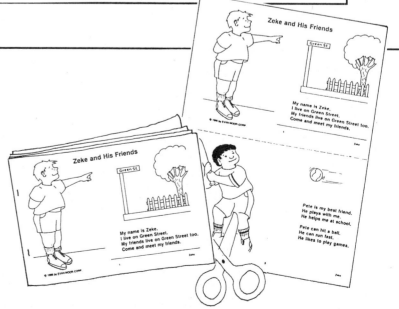

name

Fold and paste

Fold and paste

are	Aunt	ball	been
boys	come	dirt	do
down	eat	faster	find
fire	for	friends	from
funny	girls	have	her
live	look	my	

next	oh	park	party
play	put	said	saw
school	start	than	the
this	tire	to	too
twins	them	where	yelled
you	yard		

Zeke and His Friends

My name is Zeke.
I live on Green Street.
My friends live on Green Street too.
Come and meet my friends.

1

Zeke

Pete is my best friend.
He plays with me.
He helps me at school.

Pete can hit a ball.
He can run fast.
He likes to play games.

3

Zeke

Lee likes to have fun.
He rides his bike a lot.
He likes to go on skates too.

He tells the best jokes.
His jokes are funny.

2 Zeke

Kate just came to Green Street.
She is in my class at school.
She can play the flute.
She wants to be in the school band.

4 Zeke

Kate has a dog.
His name is Mike.
Mike wants to go to school with Kate.

5

Zeke

June and Eve are twins.
It is fun to play with June.
June can think of funny games to play.

7

Zeke

It is fun to play with Eve too.
She lets us all ride her bike.

June likes to help her friends.
Eve likes to tell us what to do.

6

Zeke

Will you come and play with us?

8

Zeke

Kate

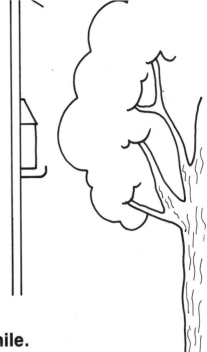

Kate put on a smile.
"I will be brave.
I will go in and meet the class.
I hope the boys and girls like me."

1

"I will help Kate in class," said June.
"And I will take her to the school yard."
"I will help her too," said Lee.
"I will tell Kate the school rules."

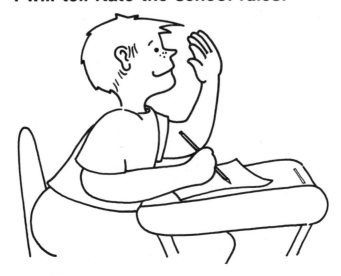

3

Miss Lane said, "This is Kate.
She will sit next to June.
Let's make Kate feel at home."

    2   Kate

The bell rang.
The boys and girls went out to play.
"What do you like to play, Kate?" asked Zeke.

"I like to go down the slide," said Kate.
"I like to play games.
I like to play ball too.
I cannot run fast, but I can hit the ball."

    4   Kate

"I like to play my flute," said Kate.

5 Kate

"This is Pete, Kate.
He is in Miss Bell's class.
Eve is in Miss Bell's class too," said Zeke.

7 Kate

"Do you have a school band?
I want to play in a band."

"We have a band," said June.
"You can be in the band when you are nine."

6

Kate

"Where do you live, Kate?" asked Pete.
"I live on Green Street," said Kate.

"June and I live on Green Street too," yelled Eve.
"We all live on Green Street!
You can play with us at school.
And you can play with us at home."

8

Kate

A Play at School

Miss Lane said, "Let's have a play."

"I want to be in the play," yelled Lee.
"Me too," said Zeke.

1

A Play

"I am fast.
I hop down the road.
I can go faster than you."

3

A Play

"Can you come to school, Dad?" asked Lee.
"You and Mom can see me in a play.
It will be fun."

"We will come to school," said Dad.
"We want to see you in a play."

"I cannot go fast,
but I will race you.
I think I will win."

"1, 2, 3, go!" said Pete.

"I did not go fast,
but I did win the race."

"I will take a nap.
I can sleep by this tree.
He is not fast.
I will still win the race."

"This was a funny play," said Dad.
"It was fun to see Lee in the play."

June and Eve

Kate went to Green Park.
She saw Pete and Zeke.
"Where are June and Eve?" asked Kate.
"I want to play with them."

1

June put beet seeds in the hole.
She put dirt on the seeds.
She gave the dirt a pat.
"I like to help," said June.
"I like to plant seeds."

3

"June and Eve have to help at home," said Zeke.
"You can play with Pete and me."

2 June and Eve

Eve dug up the weeds.
She put the weeds in a pile.
"I like to help too," said Eve.
"But I do not like to dig up the weeds."

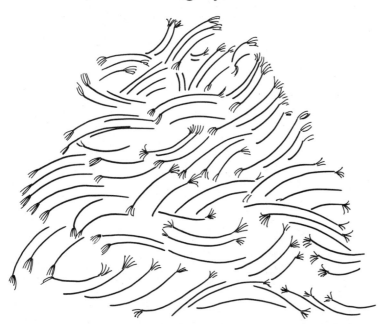

4 June and Eve

"Look at that pile of dirt," said June.
"A mole made it," said Eve.
"The mole digs in the dirt to get bugs to eat."

"You can rest if you want to," said June.
"I need to dig a hole.
This vine needs a stake."

"It is hot," said Eve.
"Let's rest."

"Let's see if Mom will make us a snack," said Eve.
"Let's go to Green Street Park to eat the snack," said June.
"I like to help, but I like to play too."

Pets at School

"Wake up, Eve," said June.
"Miss Lane said that pets can come to school.
I do not want to be late."

1 Pets

"I have pet mice," said Zeke.
"My mom and dad gave the mice to me.
My mice are white with black spots.
Mice like to eat seeds.
It is fun to have three mice for pets."

3 Pets

"This is my pet cat," said June.
"His name is Stan.
He likes to run and play.
He likes to take naps on my bed.
It is fun to have a cat for a pet."

2

Pets

"This is my dog, Mike," said Kate.
"Sit, Mike. Shake my hand.
He wants a bone to eat.
It is fun to have a dog for a pet."

4

Pets

Miss Lane had a pet too.
It was long and black.

5

"I do not have a pet," said Lee.
"I like June's cat.
I like Zeke's mice.
I like Kate's dog,
but I like Miss Lane's snake best.
I will ask my dad to get me a snake too."

7

"This is my pet," said Miss Lane.
"It is fun to have a snake for a pet."

6

Pets

It is fun to have pets at school.

8

1, 2, 3, Go

Zeke and his friends went to Green Street Park.
Zeke, Kate, Eve, and Pete rode bikes to the park.
June and Lee had skates.

1

"That will be fun," yelled Lee.
"We must keep out of the street.
We can race on the path."

3

"Let's have a race," said Pete.
We can ride from that tree to the slide."

2

1, 2, 3, Go

"Oh, no!" said Eve.
"My tire is flat. I cannot race.
I will start the race for all of you."

4

1, 2, 3, Go

**The friends made a line on the path.
Eve yelled, "1, 2, 3, go!"**

**"That was fun," said Pete.
"Do you want to race, Eve?"**

"See how fast the bikes can go," said Eve.
"See how fast June and Lee can go.
And see how fast Mike can go.
What a funny dog!"

6

"Not this time," said Eve.
"Let's go home.
Mom will make us a snack."

8

Zeke's Party

Zeke sent a note to his friends.
The note said,

Come to 19 Green Street.
Come on June 16.
Come at 2:00.
We will have fun.
Zeke

1

Zeke's friends came to Green Street on June 16.
"Let's go to the back yard," said Zeke.
"We can play games."

3

Zeke's dad will bake a big cake.
He will make it look like a kite.
The cake and ice cream are for Zeke's party.

Mom will make hot dogs.
She will get grape pop too.

"Is it time for hot dogs and cake?" asked Lee.
Zeke and his friends went to eat.

Lee ate three hot dogs.
"You will get sick, Lee," said Eve.
"I like hot dogs," said Lee.

"It is time for my kite cake," said Zeke.
Lee ate a lot of cake.
"You will get sick," said Eve.
"I like the taste of cake," said Lee.

"Lee, you look green!" said June.
"I feel sick," said Lee.
"I want to go home!"
"I will take you home, Lee," said Zeke's dad.

Eve and June gave Zeke skates.
Lee gave him an ape.
It was a funny ape.
It had on a cape and a hat.

Kate gave him a jump rope.
Pete had made Zeke a big green plane.
"This plane can go fast," said Lee.

6   Party

"We can play with my gifts," said Zeke.
Lee had to go home,
but the rest of the friends had fun.

8   Party

The Lost Dog

Kate was sad.
Mike was lost.
He did not come home to eat.
He did not come home to sleep.
Where was Mike?

1 Dog

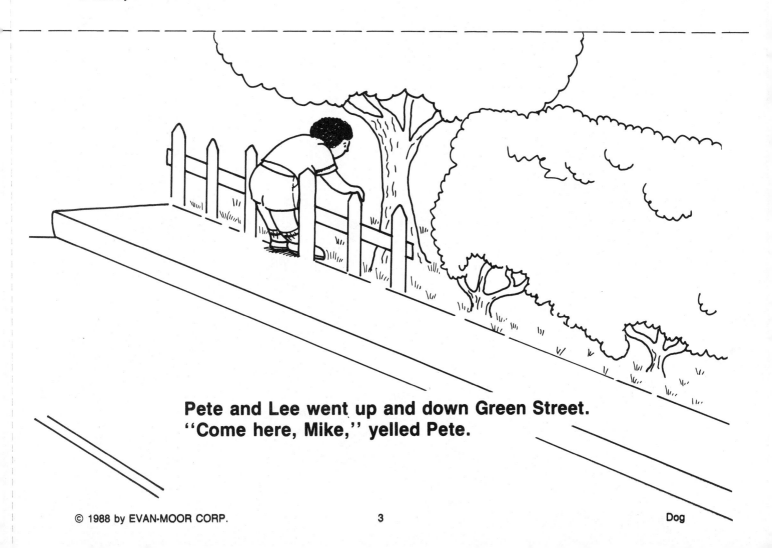

**Pete and Lee went up and down Green Street.
"Come here, Mike," yelled Pete.**

3 Dog

"We will look for Mike," said Lee.
We will look on Green Street.
We will look at school.
We will find Mike for you."

2

"Where are you, Mike?" yelled Lee.
Mike was not on Green Street.

4

June and Eve went to school.
"Come here, Mike," yelled June.
"Where are you, Mike?" yelled Eve.
Mike was not at school.

5

The dog ran to Zeke.
Zeke ran to the dog.
The black and white dog was Mike.
"Let's go home," said Zeke.

7

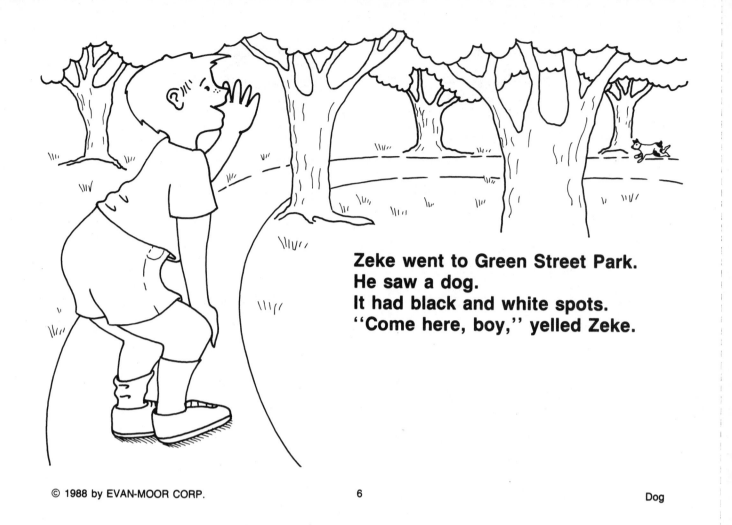

Zeke went to Green Street Park.
He saw a dog.
It had black and white spots.
"Come here, boy," yelled Zeke.

© 1988 by EVAN-MOOR CORP.

6

Dog

Kate gave Mike a big hug.
"I am glad you are home," said Kate.
"Where have you been, Mike?"
Mike just gave Kate a big kiss.

© 1988 by EVAN-MOOR CORP.

8

Dog

At the Lake

Zeke and his friends want to go to the lake.
"My Aunt Jane will take us," said Pete.

Pete's Aunt Jane has a boat.
She will take them for a ride in the boat.
The friends can fish too.

Zeke and Eve got in the boat.
Lee and Kate got in too.
Aunt Jane said, "You must sit in the boat."

"I do not like to go in a boat," said June.
"I will sit here with Mike."

"I will sit here too," said Pete.
"I can go in the boat next time."

"Can we go fast?" asked Zeke.
"We do not need to go fast to fish," said Aunt Jane.

"Will the fish bite?" asked Zeke.
"I hope I get a fish," said Eve.
"Me too," said Lee.

"I have a fish on my line," yelled Kate.
"I have a fish too," said Zeke.
The friends got nine fish.

"That is all the fish we need," said Aunt Jane.
"We will go back."

5 Lake

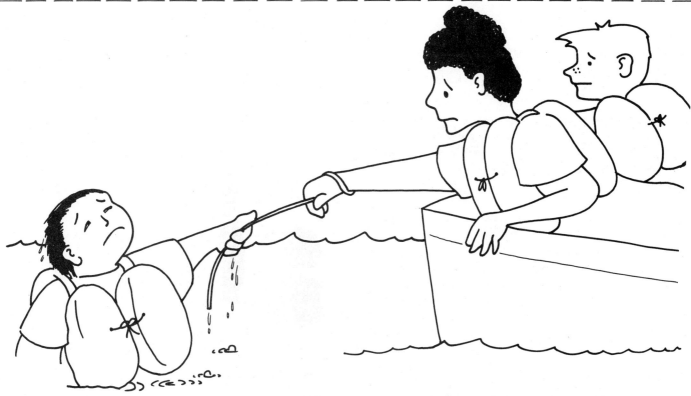

"We must save Lee," said Aunt Jane.
"Get the rope, Lee.
We will get you back in the boat."

7 Lake

Lee did not sit in the boat.
"Look out, Lee!" yelled Pete.
Lee fell into the lake.

6 Lake

Aunt Jane put her coat on Lee.
She made a big fire.
Lee sat next to the fire.

The friends ate the nine fish.
"Can we come back to the lake?" asked Lee.
"This has been fun."

8 Lake